CHEEK BY JOWL

CHEEK BY JOWL

TEN YEARS OF CELEBRATION

Simon Reade

ABSOLUTE CLASSICS

For Alison

First published in 1991 by Absolute
Classics, an imprint of Absolute Press,
14 Widcombe Crescent, Bath, England

Book Design: Peter Wilson

Phototypeset by Wyvern Typesetting,
Bristol
Printed by Longdunn Press Ltd, Bristol
Bound by Bath Press Ltd, Bath

ISBN 0 948230 47 9 Hardback
ISBN 0 948230 49 5 Paperback

CONTENTS

he first weeks of January are the low point of the British theatrical year: the contented stupor of pantomime stuns all, and critics with Sunday columns to fill try to persuade their editors to send them to Paris or New York. There was no reason to think that January 1985 was going to be any different when I turned up for the Observer at the old Donmar Warehouse to review Cheek by Jowl's Vanity Fair. The company was scarcely known, and Thackeray, cunning old thing though he is, did not lift the heart.

What was clear by the end of the evening, however, was that here was a young company of technical brilliance and elating wit, with a gift for storytelling so good that half of us wanted to read Vanity Fair at once and the other half felt they need never read it again. Pericles followed the following Monday, distinguished by a rare lucidity and by the use of musical instruments played by the actors, to sweeten a marvellously improbable story and to form a literal barrier between this world and the next.

The cheek of Cheek by Jowl then declared itself uncompromisingly and in full. In their third week at the Warehouse they gave us nothing less than the British professional première of Racine's Andromache in English, set in France around 1947, when the bitter recriminations following the Second World War perfectly matched Racine's bewildered, jealous and angry survivors of Troy. It was like watching a film noir about the Resistance and collaborators with Arletty and Daniel Gelin. We were eavesdropping as if through a lens in the room next door, and it was enthralling, both urgent and slightly absurd. This was theatre cunningly scaled to the age of the domestic screen.

Only people like Sarah Bernhardt and Marie Bell were supposed to perform plays like Andromache in England, and they performed them in large West End theatres with a melodiousness that turned them into a kind of opera without music, in which meaning was washed away by lots of lovely sound. By restoring the intimate intensity with which all seventeenth century plays were first performed, and going straight to the subject-matter of this one, which is power, passion and sex, Nick Ormerod and Declan Donnellan had walked in like angels where fools had feared to tread. (They were not quite the first to do so, but a modest spate of Racines followed theirs throughout the Eighties: Phèdre, Brittanicus, Berenice, Bajazet, another Andromache. The taboo was broken, even if the problems remain).

The extraordinary sequence of Vanity Fair, Pericles and Andromache exemplified the pattern that developed consistently over the company's first ten years: Shakespeare the core of the repertory, but matched by classics from Europe of which only one, the Philoctetes of Sophocles had ever been done here before. It is, of course, safe to say that nobody else had ever done Philoctetes with a chorus of sailors who looked as though they were on shore-leave from H.M.S. Pinafore while preserving the fury and anguish of the play intact. You're never offered the chance of a soft option with Cheek by Jowl, whatever it may feel like at the time.

Camp is the serious joker in their pack and one of the means by which Donnellan and Ormerod shock an audience with apparent incongruities while softening them up for the dramatic, essentially political, coup de grâce. For this is a political theatre company on the road, the point is often missed, which challenges injustice and received authority at every turn. The joy and importance of such a crusade in the centrist and bullyboy Eighties is one of the themes of Simon Reade's book. The ambiguities that bind tyranny with honour preoccupy the playwrights of the Spanish Golden Age and it is no coincidence that Donnellan and Ormerod's most successful venture outside Cheek by Jowl to date – Lope de Vega's Fuente Ovejuna at the National

Theatre – was immediately fed back into Donnellan's first play. In Lady Betty, his own, still scarcely explored, Irishness took Cheek by Jowl into a dangerous and thrilling poetic surrealism for the first time, and detected brave rebellion in the stomp of an Irish jig.

I was hooked by the company's fastidious fearlessness from the start and have seen every production, except the Man of Mode, since Vanity Fair. I have only been disappointed twice: a Tempest which finally collapsed under a surfeit of ideas and ingenuity which could not be matched by the movement of the plot, and a Hamlet whose intended simplicity seemed, most uncharacteristically, to give the play no firm direction or narrative shape.

The Cheek by Jowl Twelfth Night, on the other hand, in which the notorious replacement of Sir Toby's drunken catch by a tearfully bawled 'My Way' upset almost as many as it delighted, was simply the funniest, darkest and most moving of the decade (and there were many Twelfth Nights). Their Macbeth came at you like a bat out of hell; Doctor of Honour (with Lindsay Posner as guest director) placed a clean pane of glass before Calderon's chilling world; Sara transformed Lessing's morality into a gripping revenge duel; and Ostrovsky's A Family Affair was performed with the kind of exuberant rudery and physical zest more common in theatre companies from the European South and East.

In every case the acting ensemble, working together in close discipline through rehearsal and over weeks and months on tour, created a texture of mutual confidence for a masterpiece to shine through. I followed them out of London whenever possible, to Shrewsbury, Winchester, Chichester, Basildon and Kings Lynn, because Cheek by Jowl is a national theatre company and audiences from compact communities, palmed off with the second-rate for so long, are now expecting nothing but the best. Bonfires on all hilltops! Ten years of Cheek by Jowl is something to celebrate indeed.

Michael Ratcliffe

I first came across Cheek by Jowl while at University, by dashing up the A303 to London in a clapped-out Renault 4. Their production made me realise why I loved theatre − to scrutinise it, to be involved in it, to make a career associated with it − because it was a live spectacle made into a thrilling experience, in a gutsy, theatrical way.

On leaving University, I launched myself into theatre journalism, and, by happy coincidence, my first commission (from Peter Roberts, the tireless editor of *Plays International*) was to interview Declan Donnellan.

Off I went one Autumn evening to a house in Primrose Hill (everyone who has been there talks of it affectionately, especially now that it's been sold) − the door was answered by an enigmatic Nick Ormerod which temporarily confused me − and I spent three hours getting very drunk on some cheerful red wine, while being impressed by the charm, anecdotal irreverence, and wide-ranging discourse of one of my favourite directors.

So, some years later, when Peter Roberts sent me to interview Jon Croft − the innovative publisher of dashing young translations of European classics − and the interviewee casually slipped into conversation that he wished to expand his publishing interests with books about theatre, with one celebrating the first ten years of Cheek by Jowl perhaps, I presumptuously wrote to him the next day, saying that I might be just the person to write that book.

I heard nothing. Until January 1991. Arriving home on a Friday evening after another ambitious day at the Gate Theatre in Notting Hill (where I had been taken on as Literary Manager, and where I continue to work amid all the excitement and expansion of a tiny theatre dedicated to the enormousness of world drama) my answer-phone was flashing with a message from Jon Croft, saying that the Cheek by Jowl book he'd mentioned was now in my hands. The following Monday I was watching improvisations and re-rehearsals of *Hamlet*, the company miraculously releasing yet more imaginative impulses, despite being near the end of a mammoth world tour (they'd just

finished at the Lyric Hammersmith, and only had a few performances left in Greece and Hong Kong).

Researching the book which, from the perspective of its anniversary, charts the first ten years of this blooming company – from a small-scale, nine-week tour of *The Country Wife* in 1981 to a middle-scale, nine month tour of *As You Like It* from 1991–1992 – has confirmed the exhilaration I had as a student: that here was a great company in a decade of not so good British theatre. Naughtily taking on the ugly spirit of Thatcherism, they made work for themselves when no-one else would offer it to them, and were pushy enough to make the Arts and British Councils aware of their innovative talents, securing essential funding and international touring dates. It's hardly surprising that they've won a clutch of awards along the way. Their own history is special; their context in the 1980's fascinating. And I like what they do best: make a play into a theatrical celebration, an event.

By giving space to a wide variety of voices, I hope to give a thorough impression of the company. Though because theatre exists in the present and requires an intangible appreciation more than a critical response, no book on theatre could ever claim to be definitive.

Everyone who has spoken has done so enthusiastically – all the errors and misrepresentations are mine alone. As well as meeting many of the performers who have worked with Cheek by Jowl – all of whom have made an invaluable contribution to the tone of the writing while having their own say too – Jane Gibson, Nick Dear, Lindsay Posner, Richard Eyre and Sam Wanamaker have also discussed their association with Declan Donnellan and Nick Ormerod (the founding fathers of Cheek by Jowl) as have Alec Pattison of the British Council and Dan Furst by letter from Japan. While I was writing this book, Donnellan and Ormerod invited me to attend two days of a five-day location shoot of their first ever film: an eleven minute feature, set in Ealing, made for Channel 4. The producers, Impact Pictures, and the production crew gave me valuable thoughts on these new boys to film.

Declan Donnellan and Nick Ormerod, together with Cheek by Jowl's energetic Administrative Director, Barbara Matthews, and Associate Director, the composer Paddy Cunneen, have been extraordinarily welcoming and a guiding influence. Ruth Ingledow, Cheek by Jowl's PR & Marketing Officer, has helped considerably in rooting out the bulk of research material.

Much of that has been hordes of press cuttings from all around the world, which feature in this book both for their succinct appraisal of productions (which I distinguish from the plays, the scripts) and as an illustration of the effect Cheek by Jowl has had on the world's theatre community. I am indebted to all those theatre critics.

Dominic Dromgoole, Ian MacNeil, Mary Peate and Nick Sweeting provided me with interesting ideas. Michael Coveney entered into a challenging and clever debate about Cheek by Jowl, and I must acknowledge the role he has played in synthesising my ideas. Tom Sutcliffe gave me a fine perspective on Donnellan and Ormerod's opera work.

Practical help came from Jon Bryant – translating the copious press reviews from Latin America and the Iberian Peninsula – Alex Allan, and Maria Evans, Assistant Administrator of Cheek by Jowl. Stephen Daldry and Caroline Maude, my colleagues at the Gate Theatre, have been extremely understanding during the swift writing process.

Without the cajoling from the nicest publisher in Bath, Jon Croft, I wouldn't have enjoyed myself so much – and I must thank his assistant Nicki Morris for reassuring me that what he said was usually ironic.

Finally, the mundane chores, the constant support and encouragement, the neverending flow of thoughts, and the insight into performance, have come from Alison Reid, a more meticulous researcher you couldn't wish for.

Simon Reade
London
1991

he company tries to lay the text and the action open to public scrutiny. They aim at an emotional continuity between actors and audience and a fresh accessibility which gives fire to the dry tinder of the text (*Warwick Midweek* 15/3/89)

Cheek by Jowl is a name to conjure with. All over the world, people have been attempting to define the company who will grab at anything and can embrace everything, bringing the best into the closest of intimate relationships to create vibrant, public theatre. They're known as *Za pan Brat* in Poland; the Brazilians call them *Rosto a Rosto* (face to face); in Argentina, *Codo con Codo* (elbow to elbow); in Uruguay, *Hombro con Hombro* (shoulder to shoulder); while in Spain they've been dubbed *Carne y Una* (flesh and nail). Someone, somewhere, even called them 'Arse in Knickers'.

Clearly, there's something physical about Cheek by Jowl: grunting and sweating, rough and ready, brazen and exuberant. Yet there's a sensitivity in the muscularity. Their choice of some of the world's greatest drama has shown them to be refined, graceful, considerate and astute, disciplined in their intricacy. Their popularity throughout the world – from Aberdeen to Zwolle, Bombay to Bratislava, Kathmandu to Kyoto, Perth to Peshawar, Wakefield

to Warsaw – is because earthiness is coupled with finesse. Their productions reek of vulgarity *and* have an aroma as holy as the mass. Opposites, contrasts, and an ironic paradox, can all exist side by side.

Uniquely led by a director and designer, the co-artistic directors Declan Donnellan and Nick Ormerod, Cheek by Jowl's tender grappling begins with those two; they continue with the actors in rehearsal; then between the company and the text (and the text and its traditional interpretations). And finally, and most importantly, the production is brought before its audience, cheek by jowl.

There's a tiny irony – given that their re-creation of classic plays puts the words before the received opinions – that 'cheek by jowl' should come from a moment in *A Midsummer Night's Dream* when Lysander and Demetrius are trying to outvie each other in their exits:

> Lysander: *Now follow – if thou darest – to try whose right*
> *Of thine or mine is most in Helena.*
> Demetrius: *Follow? Nay, I'll go with thee, cheek by jowl (IIIii).*

There might be struggle and confrontation in a Cheek by Jowl production, but it's certainly not that of two lads bickering over who should get the girl. Though, like Demetrius' protestation, there's no-one who leads, no-one who follows in a Cheek by Jowl production. All participants go together in a world of the imagination.

There's a spirit in Cheek by Jowl which is intimate but raucous, private yet public, cerebral yet celebratory. They play with a play, make theatre in a theatre, dramatise the dramatic. They present the grotesque as the beautiful, the austere as the warm, the distorted as the focused. Never shy, never cynical, their productions celebrate both the play and the art of theatre itself. Theirs is the regeneration game, the fruition of impulses from a collective creative imagination. And, amazingly, they've done it cheek by jowl with the inhospitable eighties. Cheek by Jowl's ten years of celebration has been feted all along its world-touring way:

'Like the master art restorer who cleanses away centuries of varnish and grime to revive the blazing colours that a great painting had when it was new, Cheek by Jowl creates in each play the illusion that these events have never happened before, and may not happen now – and if they do, they cannot be controlled or forseen' (Dan Furst *Konsai Time Out* October 1990 Japan).

e did invite current undergraduates to submit tapes of their work, but ... none reached a very high standard of promise.' My goodness, he should have seen the production of *The Alchemist* produced by the undergraduate Declan Donnellan (now of Cheek by Jowl). The set consisted of two pictures the size of dinner plates, hung on an acre of black drapes. It was promise-free (Griff Rhys Jones *Times* 24/1/90, reporting Stephen Sondheim's inaugural lecture as Oxford University's first Cameron Mackintosh Professor of Drama)

Declan Donnellan and Nick Ormerod met as students at Cambridge University in the 1970's and have worked and lived together ever since. Ormerod read law, and Donnellan, thanks to the transfer possibilities of that university's Tripos system, switched to law in his third year after two years of English. Both went on to be called to the bar. Ormerod left the legal profession immediately – Donnellan left after six months pupillage. Performing for the Establishment just wasn't their cup of tea.

Neither seem typical of the Oxbridge graduate who litters the theatrical profession (as most others) since neither espouse the tradition of theatre as English literature which influences productions throughout Britain. And they're both very affable and extremely funny. Remarkably for a profession renowned for its insincerity, many who work with them become intimate personal friends.

After waving goodbye to the judges, Ormerod was quite successful in being employed as a theatre designer on various productions. Donnellan's early Fringe direction was spotted by Lisle Jones, who ran the drama course at the Arts Educational School. Subsequently Jones invited Donnellan to teach at Arts Ed. Donnellan also enjoyed improvising with the Activists at the Royal Court. But within the wider world of British theatre he was making no headway at all as he traipsed from one grey provin-

cial railway station to another, in search of some rep. manager to give him a break as a director.

So, out of a hunger for work, Donnellan and Ormerod continued to produce the odd play on the London Fringe with unpaid actors, culminating in a production of *'Tis Pity She's a Whore* at the end of 1980 in Theatre Space, a venue in the mortuary beneath an old hospital off Trafalgar Square, run by Anne Fenn, an indefatigable supporter of young companies. Shrewdly, they invited all their friends, and friends of friends, and anyone who didn't know them, who might be able to help them set up a company which would tour Britain and keep them employed in the work they loved most and which they happened to be very good at: introducing theatre audiences to refreshing appraisals of classic plays, both the ones we wouldn't know, and the ones we thought we knew until we heard and saw them reclaimed.

It is a salutary thought that only ten years ago, with as little experience as Ormerod and Donnellan actually had, on the strength of potential demonstrated in one production (their other Fringe efforts hadn't caught anyone's attention), the Arts Council would award a grant enabling the foundation of a small-scale touring company. The late Ruth Marks, responsible for promoting and championing some of the best of 1980's touring theatre from within the Arts Council, encouraged them to put in an application. With their sights set on a nine week tour of *The Country Wife* to be launched from Edinburgh, they filled in the forms, thinking up the name Cheek by Jowl the day before the application was submitted.

Nick Ormerod, at that stage, was responsible for setting up the tour:

'To satisfy the Arts Council, you had to book your tour first. After writing a bogus letter, and sending it to 250 venues, I went to see Ruth, and she said: "You don't expect them to reply do you? You've got to get on the telephone". So, after about six weeks, I patched together a feasible Autumn tour – this was March – selling *The Country Wife* for £250 a performance, which seemed a phenomenal amount of money'.

They were awarded £6,000 by the Arts Council Touring Department (and £1,154 from the Scottish

Arts Council) in exchange for 49 performances. (For the year 1991–1992, as an Arts Council Drama Department annual client, they have been awarded £90,000 in exchange for seven weeks middle-scale touring at Arts Council approved venues.)

Ruth Marks had recommended that the new Cheek by Jowl should put themselves in the hands of an arts promotion operation to produce their first play. There were a few teething problems, as there would be with any fledgling touring company, and so the two parted halfway through the *Country Wife* tour. Cheek by Jowl were momentarily left to their own inexpert devices. A former barrister turned theatre designer, Ormerod the tour planner now became a company administrator overnight.

Ormerod enjoyed the work, despite the frustrations, but he knew that his talents really lay elsewhere. (No-one can accuse him of a lack of ambition. One of his greatest hopes is to one day have a crack at acting again – he performed at Cambridge – fascinated as he is with the whole process of rehearsing. He doesn't think his return to the stage will be with Cheek by Jowl, however.) So, into the picture came Barbara Matthews. As a development of her National Student Theatre Company experience, she'd set up a theatre company with two friends, who had mounted a production at the Theatre Space venue shortly after she'd finished a postgraduate Arts Administration course at City University. The play presented was *Twelfth Night*, and a man who also fancied himself as an actor answered a newspaper advert, and was duly cast as Orsino. That man was Declan Donnellan. 'A little bit later I noticed that the same venue were doing *'Tis Pity She's a Whore*,' recounts Matthews,

'and I recognised Declan's name as the director. I went to see it and was bowled over by it. We weren't great mates at all – he was just someone I'd worked with. I wrote them a fan letter and then heard little more until Nick and Declan came to see me on my birthday, to ask me to be their administrator. Because the previous relationship with an administration company had not been terribly successful, they decided that they wanted one administrator who believed in what they were doing'.

Matthews had just taken up the post of Market-

ing Officer with Opera 80, which was a contract of only six months a year. Opera 80 generously suggested that she might want to run Cheek by Jowl from their offices and thus be available free of charge for the other six months of the year as well. Opera 80 provided Cheek by Jowl with a desk and telephone that they couldn't have afforded by themselves. This co-existence lasted for a fruitful five years.

'Cheek by Jowl gave me 10% of the bookings to start with; until eventually they noticed that I was getting too rich too quickly', says Matthews. Though she started in Autumn 1981, Matthews' efforts were strictly directed towards the next tour of *Othello* – Ormerod picking up the pieces and tying up the loose ends of *The Country Wife*, while easing Matthews into her formidable job – and transforming Cheek by Jowl from a partnership with a £6,000 overdraft facility guaranteed by Donnellan and Ormerod's house, to a non-profit distributing company limited by guarantee. This trio of Ormerod, Donnellan and Matthews is still together ten years on. And this despite not playing Horsham. 'I made the most appalling balls-up on that,' admits Matthews:

'*Othello* really was a bitty tour of one night stands – when I look at all the venues we played at, it's unbelievable what we achieved. One week we were due to play a Tuesday out in the sticks, Thursday at Christ's Hospital in Horsham, and Saturday at the Battersea Arts Centre. I'd typed out the schedule all efficiently, but I hadn't indicated the days, just the dates. It's very easy to push one key and not another. So, I'd actually typed the Friday date and not Thursday's. I knew it was Thursday. I just thought everyone else knew it was Thursday.

'The Company Manager rang me on the Thursday morning about something really trivial, and I said: "James, why haven't you left for Horsham?" – "That's tomorrow" – "No it's not. It's today" – "Oh my God". We found the entire company ... except for the actor who'd got the van. He didn't live in London, and used to take the van and stay with a different friend every night. I had to 'phone Horsham and say: "Terribly sorry. We can't find the actor with the set". They didn't talk to me for three years after that'.

Out of the 1,550 scheduled performances from *The Country Wife* to *Hamlet*, Matthews has only had to cancel three further performances owing to illness (the *Sara* company struggled on in Montevideo despite an epidemic of salmonella) and one because the van broke down, in the entire ten years. Nothing will stop the Cheek by Jowl bandwagon. Not even the coups, riots and revolutions that have accompanied or followed their performances (and lead one to ponder what theories about late twentieth century world events future historians will come up with: looking for something more tenable than a chaos theory, they might well chart the events of the 1980's and 1990's along the route taken by Cheek by Jowl's tours and the profound effect their theatre has left in its wake – the Cheek by Jowl actor Keith Bartlett thinks he's rumbled them: 'Nick and Declan actually work for the CIA. Cheek by Jowl is just a front').

British and international touring has been at the root of the company. The classic plays that they choose are partly informed by Donnellan and Ormerod's instinct that they will grow on tour for the actors. There's nothing worse than being on the road for eighteen months with a stodgy, intransigent play. Classics are organic plays, altering as the performers discover new nuances, new rhythms, that have been latent in the script. The style of a Cheek by Jowl production (less of a specific house style when the choice of plays is so varied; more of a distinctive atmosphere) contributes to this expansive process. Theatre theoreticians are often miffed when seeking out the prompt copy of a Cheek by Jowl Shakespeare, only to discover that where performances are fluid, nothing can be set. For the same reason, lighting designers have had their admirable efforts frustrated, as actors might change their performances, even their blocking, so that where a clever red gel worked in one performance, it just looks daft and out of place in the next.

Ormerod (a naturally diffident man with strangers) can get embarrassed on tour when an in-house sparks speaks loudly in amazement that he should get a Lighting Design credit in the programme, since Ormerod quickly exposes himself to be ignorant of the mechanics, only a craftsman with

Krieg...

Der Bearbeitung durc...
Gründer dieser Theater...
Declan Donnellan und...
Ormerod ist anzume...
chen Spaß sie bei de...
habt haben. Da ne...
gerne hin, daß in...
szenierung das...
ment — wie Simo...
tausch (Simo...
nicht nur S...
dern auch...
Pauline)...
rückt.

provvisazioni, riferimenti

ne gruppo ha offerto in pri...

olare allestimento del dramm...

premier inglese in regina di Na...

Bler...
schen...
ebens...
chen...
mir...
Oh...
o...
to...
co...
dati...
sso...

...elia (Amanda Harris) mit ihrem we-
Bild: Cheek
...Duncan Bell).

Ur...

Chi conosce i Jowl», la giovan britannica, nata s... venuta per la pr... Itaña, proprio a... Taormina, tre a... un'indimenticabil... kespeariano che... t'oggi il loro migli... lo, non poteva cer... dalla nuova mess... lettura tradiziona... ma elisabettiano. Nella *Dodicesima* anni fa, avevano... più bello, *My Way*...

e Rivalinnen
Jahrmarkt der Eitelkeiten

...", die tik ist schließlich eine Domäne
...l in der des britischen Theaters.
...lle kul-
...bietet, ge-
...Theater-
...die Auf-
...ner Tour-
...Cheek by
...

Man kennt sie alle, die Typer die um die Jugendfreundinn... Amelia und Rebecca kreisen sowie und an deren wechselvollem Schicksal teilhaben: Liebeswer-ben, Enterbung, Komödie aber auch Tragödie der Liebe. Rivali-täten unter den Freundinnen. ...llarvt wird die ganze Skala Schwächen, zw ...her ...mehr Verständ-...

17 GIO
GIO

La Che...

se... na... ro...

...INA — ... spirito ... Shakes... dolo sol...

stumi, in quell... gioco ironico nei riguar-di dell'attuale governo Thatcher, la Cheek By Jowl Company ritorna a Taormina con un'altra opera shakespeariana, «La tempesta».

Lo spettacolo, penulti-mo lavoro teatrale a Taormina Arte che chiu-derà con il «Liolà» di Gigi Proietti, debutterà que-sta sera in prima assolu-ta alla Villa comunale (repliche sino a sabato), nel medesimo luogo che aveva visto la giovane compagnia inglese prota-gonista di altre due opere shakespeariane: «Il so-gno di una notte di mezza estate» e «La dodicesima notte».

«La scena sarà vuota all'inizio» — dice il giova-ne regista inglese Declan Donnellan — «poi come ...dia dell'ar...

un mondo utopistico, abitato da Calibano e da Ariel, lasciandosi alle spalle un mondo anar-chico che per me è rap-presentato dal giuoco del potere di quel tempo».

«Il nostro» — è sempre Donnellan a parlare — «è un teatro di poesia, non didascalico alla maniera di Brecht e il tutto dev avvenire come in un so-gno... poi gli spettato vedano ciò che voglior vedere».

Gli attori della com-pagnia «Cheek By Jowl» no dodici e fra qu vanno segnalati A White (la perfida re di Napoli), Keith Bar (Stefano), Timothy ker (Prospero). La sc grafia e i costumi so Nick Ormerod, le che di Paddy Cunne

I Cheek By Jow al repertorio shak ... si rico...

begavet
humor

...eek by Jowls opførelse af
...akespeares »Twelfth Night« er
...rhjernet, smuk og vittig

...dens intriger, seksuelle.
...mper og sociale rollespil
...tydeligt, skønt uhøjtide-
...Declan Donnellans
...nesættelse har et lystigt,
...da løssluppent, men
...ttra letfærdigt forhold
...Shakespeare, og fysisk
...erer han raffineret pe-
...ne i skiftende diagona-
...hen over sceneguivet.
...s iscenesættelse er præ-
...af megen følsomhed,
...også af en skakspillers
...je klogt.
...medvirkende...

veloplagt, præcist og bega-vet. Og det fornemmes ikke som et påklistret stilbrud, når £eks. Sinatra-sangen ›My Way‹ indgår i forestil-lingen. Bare en gang? Nej more, much more than this.

Opførelsen i Østre Gas-værk af ›Twelfth Night‹ er både smuk, komisk, lyrisk, psykologisk træfsikkel uhyre klarhjernet. For lingen burde spilles langt flere gange, end d tilfældet...

...r e...
se...
h...

od kind
VI...

Parodistica citazione della La...

Servizio di
Pier Cardinali

TAORMINA —Fin dall'inizio lo spettacolo scopre le carte: la tempesta che apre l'azione è mimata da un gruppo di attori, in abiti moderni, che dalla pla-tea salgono sul palcoscenico, richiamati da Prospero - capo-comico per rappresentare pin nota intuizione critica di randellianamente (secondo la Kott in *Shakespeare nostro contemporaneo*) una improv-visazione sul tema dell'utopia. Evitando i luoghi comuni del-l'interpretazione paludata, monumentale, «memorabile, (come sem...

Sferzate s

quotidiana

a Taormina

ha trasform...

Sonho de Uma Noite de Verão, na Sala Villa- do Teatro Nacio-nal.

O grande trunfo dessa monta-gem está na roupagem atual que o texto clássico recebeu. Sem cenários — apenas um pa-no branco colocado no chão — e sem figurinos de épocas, as per-sonagens shakespearianas se deslocam num mundo mágico ligado aos dias de hoje. Nada é por acaso: os atores se vestem com calças jeans, camisetas, bonés e botas verdes para os no-bres. Um verdadeiro estudo do feitiço. O texto é mantido no ori-ginal e os climas necessários à trama são criados através de uma iluminação competente e na própria concentração das re-lações entre as diversas perso-nagens.

Em cena, dez atores — cinco homens e cinco mulheres — vi-vem as aventuras e desventu-ras de mortais e imortais. A es-tória se desenrola na Antigüida-de, quando Theseus, Duque de

...decidir-se, mas era e Lysander planejam uma fuga secreta pe-la floresta. Demetrius descobre o plano e decide segui-los, jun-tamente com Helena. Ao mes-mo tempo, um grupo de traba-lhadores de Atenas, chefiado pelo falante Botton, apresenta-rá uma peça teatral na corte de Theseus em homenagem a seu casamento. O grupo, então deci-de ensaiar na floresta. E é jus-tamente no cenário da floresta, onde moram as fadas e os duen-des, que a ação se desenrola, contando com a magia de Obe-ron, Rei dos Imortais, e de Tita-nia, Rainha dos Imortais.

Na trama, todos os ingredien-tes necessários para que um rit-mo acelerado aconteça. Cheek by Jowl — que quer dizer "lado a lado" — procura, com isso, di-vulgar os grandes nomes da dramaturgia inglesa, além, é claro, de mostrar um bom tra-balho teatral sem a parafernã-lia característica à montagem dos textos clássicos. Assim, o público poderá se delicar com as palavras de William Shekes-

CARLOS JACOBINA

ta, persino all'improv-ne.

-Shakespeare nei suoi metteva canzoni e...

the poetry – the pictures rather than the LX practice. Where all artistic efforts are directed towards the actor, a Cheek by Jowl lighting designer too can be there all the time to develop the design from the beginning of rehearsals (which is generally an unreasonable demand in the profession). Cheek by Jowl hasn't always been happy with a lighting designer being brought in at the last moment. So the Ormerod/Stage Manager lighting design has often proved the most satisfactory to Cheek by Jowl, while sometimes being baited for its unorthodoxy by the regional reps.

Cheek by Jowl's first foreign tour, which happened at the same time as *Othello* toured Britain, was with a double-bill of Barrie Keefe's *Gotcha* and a simple musical, set in a boarding school, *Rack Abbey* (by Donnellan and Colin Sell). Cheek by Jowl now recognise that this piece, mainly for schools' audiences, was not strictly part of its repertory – though they do still have a mountain of school-science test-tubes in their store-room should a revival ever materialise. Smattered with cod public school jargon, the very opposite of Keefe's *Gotcha*, *Rack Abbey* is a flimsy satire of toffs and nutters, school bullies, adolescent crushes on school maids, a Tom Brown/Flashman initiation of a New Boy, with a preposterous ghost-story thrown in. It is unashamedly light-hearted. Yet, paired with *Gotcha*, it must have raised serious questions abroad about Britain's divisive education system. And, as Donnellan argues in the published play's introduction, it is a portrait of a powerful British class. *Rack Abbey*, his introduction claims, is:

> 'Hardly a caricature, and its pupils will govern Britain for some time to come'.

The tour came about because of an inspired Dutch impresario, and though successful for its type, it was never seen outside the Low Countries.

The British Council did have some influence on that tour, but they really got onto Cheek by Jowl's case by enabling their first official invitation abroad for their third and fourth productions, *Vanity Fair* and *Pericles*, from the Jerusalem Festival in the Autumn of 1984. (Babs Todd, recently of RADA and on Cheek by Jowl's Development Panel, had been instrumental in the initial *Gotcha/Rack Abbey* visit: she'd seen late rehearsals of these plays and

diplomatically offered the company an extra £800 if they promised to continue rehearsing for an extra week – the British Council's first financial contribution to Cheek by Jowl.)

Back in Britain, it was the small-scale touring that was gaining Cheek by Jowl a reputation. Other companies like Shared Experience, Actors Touring Company and Cherub had been touting similar work. One of Donnellan's first influences, along with the early work of Joint Stock and some of the more innovative dance companies, was Shared Experience's Mike Alfreds:

> 'Theatre isn't always a very good world for making people feel welcome. But we had tremendous encouragement from Mike Alfreds at the beginning. We're grateful for that, because he never made us feel that we were muscling in'.

Shared Experience, and other companies like Monstrous Regiment, had captured the imagination of audiences and critics that Cheek by Jowl were about to build upon in a massive way. But as other companies lost their impetus as their artistic leaders departed – unable to capitalise on what they had created for themselves, content to tour the same small-scale circuits year after year, rather than look wider or think bigger – Cheek by Jowl had consistent ambition, able to grow with the stability of the same company core of Matthews, Ormerod

and Donnellan, persistently expanding their choice of venues as they recognised the potential audience across Britain. 'When we started,' says Donnellan,

'it was to tour an ensemble theatre and to break down some of the barriers that had started to exist between modern audiences and classical plays. We weren't the only company doing that, but we too wanted to examine the plays for now in a very fresh way'.

For *The Country Wife* and *Othello*, London dates had been a mixture of one-night stands and rushed weeks here and there – at Theatre Space, Hampstead's New End theatre, Battersea Arts Centre and Jackson's Lane. By the end of its first decade, Cheek by Jowl could play Hammersmith's Lyric Theatre, the Almeida, and the Lilian Baylis. The real turning point had come when Nica Burns, running the Donmar Warehouse off Covent Garden, had the foresight to programme Cheek by Jowl's triple bill of *Vanity Fair*, *Pericles* and *Andromache* into the commercially quiet time of the New Year in 1985. They're not three plays which, at face value, have a festive, seasonal spirit. Barbara Matthews takes up the story:

'Because we had a young company – a lot of them were straight out of drama school – we were able to keep them together for eighteen months, keeping their creativity flourishing by adding plays to

their repertoire. We hadn't brought any of the three plays, which shared the same casts, to London. We'd just been touring round the world, and to village halls, and just about everywhere else, except London. Nica Burns offered us a three week run at the very beginning of January (we'd started *Vanity Fair* at the Bedlam Theatre on the Edinburgh Festival Fringe eighteen months before). We didn't know that opening in January was actually a shrewd thing to do because nobody else in their right mind opens in January – they've all had their shows up in time for Christmas. The wonderful thing about the Donmar Warehouse was that it was almost a West End theatre, so the critics took it seriously. Being January, the critics had little else to do but take up the offer of press tickets on a press release from a company they hadn't really heard of before, with a stupid name, that was doing a British premiere of *Andromache*, an obscure old Shakespeare of interest to the Shakespeare collectors only, and *Vanity Fair* which was only an adaptation. On the other hand, perhaps the whole venture was a bit fascinating for them. We got the most phenomenal attendance from the national critics and they gave us wonderful reviews. We sold out, we made money, and our careers were seriously launched. And then we won the Laurence Olivier Award for that season. That gave us the status to start booking two or three nights at the Warwick Arts Centres. Gone were the days of the one-night stand. And I think as a result we had more offers from abroad'.

One such offer came from Uruguay, where *A Midsummer Night's Dream*, their sixth production and first uproarious Shakespeare comedy, played at the Millington Drake Theatre in April 1985, as part of the Montevideo Festival (a celebration organised by the national critics, who are benign enough not to publish their reviews of the Festival's productions until it is all over and the companies have returned home). It was a tremendous hit. As the lights faded at the end of the first performance, there was an extraordinary rumble as the audience rose to its feet to greet the actors with an ecstatic roar in the curtain-call. *A Midsummer Night's Dream* was probably the first production in which Matthews had some sort of artistic influence: she'd mentioned it in passing as Cheek by Jowl were wondering how to follow up their previous success – and thus made her own life easier as this play has more marketable appeal than an obscure European classic.

One would have thought that 'Cheek by Jowl' itself would be enough to sell a show by this stage, and since Iain Lanyon gave them their distinctive logo in 1983 – which Lanyon claims to have doodled on the back of an envelope while travelling by tube for a meeting with Matthews – a 'stamp' which features on all their publicity material (though not necessarily on their productions) Cheek by Jowl has had a clear identity. Perhaps Matthews was being overcautious. She certainly wouldn't want to dictate the artistic tastes of her two co-directors.

Since 1986, Matthews has been working from Alford House in Vauxhall, a sort of Edwardian community centre, with plenty of rehearsal spaces, which many visiting theatre companies have snootily dubbed 'Awful House' during their own rehearsals (mainly West End musicals), probably because it's located at the back of a council estate and has long dark corridors, grammar school linoleum, and an unglamorous cafeteria. Yet the rehearsal rooms are bright and spacious. And through the doors of the Cheek by Jowl offices, it's friendly and warm – the *chaise longue* in Matthews' large office, left over from *A Family Affair*, seems the height of luxury, even if it does suggest that the days of the casting couch might not be over.

Unusually for a theatre company, the Artistic Directors have no desk within this building, preferring to work from home. As a result no-one gets on top of each other, and each has a free rein. It's a relationship of mutual trust, the symbiosis of which is obviously very strong after ten years.

The composer Paddy Cunneen, a self-confessed 'late arrival at the Cheek by Jowl Ball', became the Associate Director in 1989 (after *The Tempest* and *Philoctetes*, during *Fuente Ovejuna* at the National Theatre, and before *Lady Betty*) but he realises that the title is merely a recognition of the proximity that they have in the rehearsal room rather than an appointment to an official post:

'The formula that is Nick and Declan and Barbara as the hub of Cheek by Jowl is a very good for-mula. I just contribute to it as it goes along rather than become part of that caucus. "Associate Director" is just quotation marks around a loose relationship that we have. It's much more mutual than role-play'.

Cheek by Jowl does have a Board of Directors, as any company limited by guarantee must have, which is chaired by the Edinburgh lawyer, John Scott Moncrieff (a great fan of the theatre, who Ormerod had met when working at the Edinburgh Lyceum in the late seventies). Donnellan, Ormerod and Matthews are effectively executive directors with no legal powers. The day-to-day running of the company is taken on by Matthews, who has received much recognition from other theatre administrators in the profession (she's regularly invited to give talks to the Association of Business Sponsorship of the Arts (ABSA)). Wider artistic decisions are taken on an informal basis. Donnellan and Ormerod are given the freedom of not having to observe office hours and not to have to engage in the type of paper-work that they might not be suited to, but that is so often expected of most artistic directors who super-humanly double as managers. Donnellan and Ormerod have reaped the creative benefits of being devoted to one theatre company with a coherent artistic policy, rather than freelancing around on a creatively ad hoc basis like so many of their contemporaries.

Because Matthews is the only one who is resident in the office (along with her support team) and because of her warmly embracing nature, the actors do tend to

'waltz into my office for a coffee break, trampling VAT returns underfoot as they go'

when they are rehearsing at Alford House. She has a caption on the wall above her desk to remind her that: 'An administrator is the calm in the middle of the Tempest'. Her financial brief has meant that she has had to make stark choices about plays, despite her devotion to the business serving the Art, rather than the other way round: 'My aim is to produce good theatre and not necessarily profit'. Donnellan wanted twelve performers for *Lady Betty* in 1989; Matthews could only balance the books with ten. But there are never any quarrels. She didn't need to tell them that it would be unwise to perform *Philoc-*

tetes, the recipient of the first prize in the 1988 LWT Plays on Stage Award, on its own; and because of that LWT money (£15,000) they were able to make the illuminating pairing of *Philoctetes* with *The Tempest*:

'If I say to Declan and Nick "We can't afford it", then they accept it. They don't ask: "Why? Prove it to us. Are you sure?", because they know I only say what I mean'.

Matthews has been lucky in that there have been few financial crises within the company. On the small-scale touring circuit, the performances have been virtually all paid for by the venues, backed up by the Regional Arts Associations. (Now that Cheek by Jowl tours a middle-scale circuit, it no longer receives support from the R.A.A.'s since they tend to support the venues directly.) A lot of income is generated by the international tours; the British Council, like all funding bodies, are effectively buying a service. Occasionally they have attracted sponsorship, usually in kind. And, most importantly, they have come to feel confident with the Arts Council's ongoing dedication, despite the constant fear of The Cuts.

'When launching Cheek by Jowl,' says Donnellan, 'everybody said that it was the most terrible time to start a company because there was such a recession. Later some people said that we shouldn't try to become an Equity company because we wouldn't get that kind of funding from the Arts Council. And then some suggested that we shouldn't do European classics because there wasn't a market for them'.

There is a hunger for touring theatre in the provinces. Some towns have no theatres at all. Those that do are hard-pressed to sustain permanent companies. Thus audiences devour the work of visiting companies. Michael Coveney recognises that Cheek by Jowl is an important part of the touring phenomenon:

'I suppose with the collapse of the regional reps in terms of doing anything resembling an intellectual repertoire, or Shakespeare, something like Cheek by Jowl was fulfilling that hunger for the audiences. They did address themselves to an accessible, young audience – which isn't to say that their productions weren't properly techni-

cally controlled on the whole, or well done, because they were. They made audiences feel that theatre could be exciting, glamorous and informal, which was quite a new thing. I think that was characteristic of the eighties'.

'It's much easier to do something very experimental in small-scale venues,' says Donnellan:

'Persuading mid-scale venues to take a premiere of a Lessing play for a week is more tricky. And it's marvellous that they stuck by us. It's one thing to sell one performance to a small-scale Arts Centre, but quite another to sell it to a large theatre for a week. But there is an audience for great plays'.

'Cheek by Jowl' probably put bums on seats since it is the company, not the individual shows or the individuals within the shows, who is the star. But the loyalty of venues to Cheek by Jowl has been impressive throughout the past ten years. Stephen Walton, formerly of Bury St Edmunds' Theatre Royal, a 350-seat auditorium, persisted in inviting the company to return despite initial poor box office returns: 49% for *Vanity Fair*; a shameful 19% for *Pericles*. As a long-term investment it has paid off. When *Hamlet* played a week there in September 1990, the management must have been delighted with a 90% box office.

Michael Coveney also highlights how Cheek by Jowl made themselves available to tour internationally:

'The thing you have to say about Declan and Nick is that, apart from Ian McKellen, they are the people most committed to touring. And they actually like it. I've seen them with their mini-bar in Prague, you know. They like meeting hostile critics in hotel corridors. They like being in hotels, they like travelling; they love new environments, they are very good in public relations, they like new theatres. They are genuinely excited by it. They're not boring sit-at-homes. They do want to get out there and learn and see and do it. That's a tremendous instinct'.

Touring abroad has demonstrated to Donnellan and Ormerod how poor the conditions for actors are in Britain. *Vanity Fair* once toured eighteen venues in three weeks, which must have been punishing and exhausting. 'It's a very hard life,' appreciates

Donnellan,

'and though there are a great many rewards, it's very unsettling. It does need to be paid for by the Arts Council really well. It's noticeable when we go abroad how much better it is. Bed-and-Breakfast is fine when you're on holiday. But you can't get sentimental about theatrical digs. They're not fine; your art suffers. Actors ought to be at least given the same environment as a commercial traveller'.

In appreciation of what their actors have to go through, Cheek by Jowl now rarely play Monday nights, to enable the company to have some sort of week-end after the Saturday night performance. During *Hamlet*, no matinées were programmed outside London either. And on tours abroad, the scheduling is such that the company returns home as much as possible in between foreign dates. Above all, the actors and stage managers are paid the same wage by Cheek by Jowl, each contribution valued as much as the other.

The actors constitute Cheek by Jowl at any one time, and Donnellan and Ormerod recognise the debt that the company owes to them, especially when Cheek by Jowl is usually regarded solely as the embodiment of the two Artistic Directors: 'It's unfair,' says Donnellan, 'but it happens because, apart from Barbara, we are the only constants'.

One performer who was constant during a major part of Cheek by Jowl's touring – and many do stay to be nurtured by the company for a significant number of productions – is Keith Bartlett. He puts his enjoyment of gruelling tours, from *Twelfth Night* to *The Tempest*, down to the productions inspired by Donnellan and Ormerod. Taking productions abroad, even when the language is not always understood, doesn't fall on deaf ears because the stories are presented visually:

'With the story so clear it translates into lots of different cultures. The relationships in the stories can be very complex, but Declan's very good at making sure that everyone understands. There's never anything obscure.

'A production has its own momentum on tour, but you still have at the back of your mind: "Here comes London". We try to be casual about it, but inwardly we think: "Shit!". When a show's gone well, it's good to know you're taking in a good show. There's nothing worse than touring with a bad show on a long tour. You go in and apologise before it starts'.

One of the reasons tours have worked so well – both the productions on various stages, and the company spirit off-stage – has been because of the intuitive nature of the casting, of gathering together a cohesive company.

One of the myths about Cheek by Jowl is that you can only join the company if you are also a talented musician. Paddy Cunneen points out that on the productions in which he has been involved in the casting, the musical make-up of the company has been far weaker than the cast of *As You Like It*, a production with which he had no say in casting at all, but has coincidentally discovered brass players, wind instrumentalists, a violinist and a collection of key-board and drum players amongst its numbers, and all of whom are accomplished singers.

One of the truths about Cheek by Jowl casting, is that in audition you're fine as long as Donnellan is chatting away. As soon as the more watchful Ormerod starts to chip in you know you're in trouble.

And the major moan about the casting (apart from those actresses who, recognising the opportunities Cheek by Jowl have given to women in classical roles throughout the eighties, felt betrayed that the tenth anniversary production should be all-male) is how Cheek by Jowl rely on casting directors to draw up an initial short-list. A lot of emotional time and energy is filtered by using casting directors, but some actors consider this to be unfairly exclusive.

Donnellan and Ormerod don't see all the theatre productions that have hot-tip talent performing (when they do go to the theatre, it's as members of the audience on a night off, not as talent-scouts). They won't hold open auditions, which hundreds of eager drama-school graduates would like, because they don't want to demean performers, whose art and craft they respect, by taking a cattle-market of five-minute audition speeches. Auditioning is the one thing about theatre Donnellan likes the least. He loathes having to put actors through it.

Even when they're auditioning performers whose work they know, and who might even be personal friends, the audition process is thorough, as two of those involved in *A Family Affair* in 1988 reveal.

'Before presenting them with a first draft,' explains Nick Dear,

'they asked me if I could do a couple of speeches for casting. So, I translated the first page – Declan later said that as soon as they saw the first page, they knew that they were right, they knew it was going to be okay. So they went ahead and cast it without actually seeing the script'.

Lesley Sharp auditioned for *A Family Affair*, and was asked to do that first speech:

'I had to go and read the opening speech, about how Lipochka loves dancing. I was then thrown right into it with Declan giving me advice and guiding me in the right direction'.

It's the casting of particularly youthful companies that has given Cheek by Jowl its world-touring energy. It has also contributed to the wildness of a quick-fire imagination paraded on stage.

When trying to sum up that Cheek by Jowl spirit, some have chosen to refer to the touring activities:

'The company's name implies attempts at close contact with the audience, while the fact that it is a touring company reflects its social task of propagating and spreading interest in theatre' (Grzegorz Sinko *Teatr* June 1987 Warsaw).

Edward Peters of the *Portsmouth News* (22/5/90) and Sarah Jane Checkland reporting for *The Times* from Tokyo (4/10/90 – where David Mellor, as the temporary Arts Minister became a Cheek by Jowl convert during his crash course in British culture at the UK 90 Festival) have both called Cheek by Jowl: 'The avant-garde theatre company'. Neville Hadsley in the *Birmingham Post* thought they were:

'Perhaps the most imaginative and potent theatre company to emerge in Britain in the eighties' (16/5/90).

Edward Pearce in *Encounter* fearfully described them as:

'The fashionable, critic-intimidating Cheek by Jowl company' (November 1987),

and that intimidation has even extended to their distinctive programmes designed by Iain Lanyon – large format, informative, with a photograph of the production's company and production team being jolly on a climbing frame – which eventually had a

review all of its own in 1989:

'One of the most unwieldy programmes ever offered by an usherette' (John Coldstream *Daily Telegraph* 28/4/89 Donmar Warehouse).

As the ambitious programming grew – putting *Vanity Fair*, *Pericles* and *Andromache* together in one season; *A Midsummer Night's Dream* and *The Man of Mode*; *Twelfth Night* and *The Cid* and then *Macbeth*; *The Tempest* and *Philoctetes* – Donnellan and Ormerod began to share the creative input of a Cheek by Jowl production, enlarging the artistic possibilities. Nick Dear wrote his version of *A Family Affair*; Lindsay Posner, a former assistant director with Cheek by Jowl, and designer Julian McGowan were entrusted with *The Doctor of Honour*; Jane Gibson provided essential movement for *Lady Betty*, *Sara, and Hamlet* (as well as *Fuente Ovejuna* and *Peer Gynt* at the National); Paddy Cunneen underscored *The Tempest* and *Philoctetes*, wrote the music for *Lady Betty*, and was crucial to the rehearsal development of *Sara* and *Hamlet* (working on the two National Theatre productions too). And as the shift from small- to middle-scale touring became a natural evolutionary growth, the casts, and thus the prime resources of talent, became larger too.

Cheek by Jowl has had its imitators. It is often the yard-stick by which other productions are judged or beaten. In 1988, David Edgar could talk of 'post Cheek by Jowl' productions on the stages of large theatre institutions (*Independent* 2/1/88). Not that Cheek by Jowl were necessarily the first to offer such stylish, intriguing, and celebratory productions. They were both the product and a progeniture of a *zeitgeist*, of which they themselves were at the zenith.

The consistency in the standard of Cheek by Jowl's work has ensured that by moving to the middle-scale touring circuit, they need not compromise their artistic choices. Indeed, their work in one of the largest venues of all at the National Theatre's Olivier, has shown the ability of Donnellan and Ormerod's style to transcend the limitations of space. The 1980's and beyond have proved that the 'promise-free' student director of *The Alchemist*, and its leading actor – Ormerod played Subtle – can now offer a production promise-crammed.

RESTORING THE RESTORATION

1981   **THE COUNTRY WIFE**
1982   OTHELLO
1983   VANITY FAIR
1984   PERICLES
1984   ANDROMACHE
1985   A MIDSUMMER NIGHT'S DRE.
1985   **THE MAN OF MODE**
1986   TWELFTH NIGHT
1986   THE CID
1987   MACBETH
1988   A FAMILY AFFAIR
1988   PHILOCTETES
1988   THE TEMPEST
1989   THE DOCTOR OF HONOUR
1989   LADY BETTY
1990   SARA
1990   HAMLET
1991   AS YOU LIKE IT

THE COUNTRY WIFE

estoration comedies are generally
revived with pomp and circumstance, in a welter
of wigs, fans and screens: they're designers' perfect excuse for going to town. A new touring company called Cheek by Jowl have realised
Wycherly's *The Country Wife* in a very different
manner, with three small wooden boxes, a larger
one which doubles as a sedan chair, a restaurant
and a bedroom, and sundry white garments which
allow the six actors to quick-change their way
through double that number of parts. Under
Declan Donnellan's direction theirs is a coruscat-
ing ensemble performance (Michael Church *The
Times* 9/10/81)

Thus Michael Church immediately picked up on
what were to be the distinctive hallmarks of Cheek
by Jowl. They were not just dusting away the cob-
webs from preconceived production values. They
were not out to shock with new gimmicky conceptualisations. They were not using actors as
mannequins in some bold aesthetic to precociously
draw attention to themselves. Theirs is the theatre
of the imagination, releasing actors' performances
in an unselfish, spirited ensemble. They enjoy the
texts for what they say, not what tired academics

say that they say. They present those refreshing and thrilling productions with inventive but minimal sets, allowing the performers the power to communicate with the audience, rather than dwarfing the actors to deliver undynamic, inconsequential squeaks.

The significance of Cheek by Jowl's work in the 1980's was multiple: British theatre – which saw a West End glut of mindless musicals, Shakespeare productions churn out yet more of the same large-scale subsidised sets peopled by under-used spear-carriers, and provincial playhouses decline into a quick-buck mentality by presenting the fourth generation of a West End musical/comedy/Ayckbourn – maintained its developing creativity thanks largely to companies like Cheek by Jowl who continued to explore, popularise and create new artistic interest.

With *The Country Wife*, Cheek by Jowl was a relatively impoverished theatre. But Nick Ormerod appreciates that it was, perhaps, an advantage – to make a virtue of necessity, to be pragmatic about smallness:

'There is a kind of puritanism that goes through both of us – and it's both of necessity and not – that if you want to put anything on stage it's really got to earn its place. Consequently, it ought to serve as many different functions as possible'.

Ormerod's sets aren't just scenic, but, as with *The Country Wife*, three-dimensional and mobile, incorporated into what the actors are doing. Thus the sets have to be built right up to the last moment, well into the rehearsal period. Ormerod doesn't complete their design until he has a fairly clear idea of how they will affect the flow of the action; in other words, once the production is truly taking shape.

One member of the first Cheek by Jowl company, Simon Needs (an actor who was to work with Donnellan and Ormerod again, at Exeter's Northcott Theatre in *Bent*, in 1983, and then on their National Theatre debut with *Fuente Ovejuna* at the Cottesloe Theatre in 1989) was impressed by this poor theatre at its richest. In 1981, Needs came to Cheek by Jowl with a healthy scepticism:

'I thought: "This is a dreadful name; it's going to be awful"! A friend of mine knew that they were casting *The Country Wife* and were having difficulty finding their Pinchwife. So he suggested that I went for an interview down at the Drill Hall in London. I started rehearsing the next day.

'I think Declan chatted a bit and then we all got up and started to do it straight away. I suppose he does what is obvious really. It's not at all pretentious and there's no mystique about it. He works with the script, to get the truth out of it and the actors. You don't discuss it for hours. What he does is really very practical.

'He came up with this new way of working which only suits him. I don't think another director could emulate it really. It sounds so obvious because it's what every director should do, but he'd talk to every actor completely differently because he knows what will bring out of them the qualities he wants to see. That sounds manipulative but somehow it isn't. You just opened yourself out to him, giving yourself to him.

'Nick had no budget at all for the design, but it was absolutely brilliant. The wigs were nylon and the costumes were very basic tunics, made out of calico. Though I was playing Pinchwife, I was playing Old Lady Squeamish as well. These tunics were so ingenious that you just pulled a zip and the whole thing turned into a dress. With a feather in my hat, I immediately became the woman. When we were rehearsing, Declan didn't want us to do it as a drag act. He wanted us to forget completely about playing a woman and just play the character as we saw it. We didn't put on female voices or walk as women or anything'.

They rehearsed at the Drill Hall for three weeks, on the understanding that after playing the Edinburgh Fringe Festival as an unknown company for no money at all – or profit share, if there was any, which seemed unlikely – in a 150-seat venue (a church hall at the bottom of some steep stone steps, St Columba's by the Castle) they would do a nine week tour for £80 a week, including loading and unloading the van. They had a battered Mercedes van then, and for some time after, which the actors had to drive as well. 'It was a very strange tour,' continues Needs,

'because some places we played had five or six people in the audience and we got virtually no response. At other places, like Oldham's Grange Arts Centre, we had an amazing reaction, which brought us out in tears.

'I was expecting it to be a disorganised, Fringe thing, because they obviously had no money — and often it was chaos. When we finished at Oldham on a high, I was driving the van out and was stopped by the police. The van wasn't taxed, or insured, or MOT'd, or anything. I rang Declan and had a real barney. He side-stepped the issue: "It's all Nick's fault", he said. So Nick had to come with me to the police station. From that disorganisation came a brilliant production'.

In miraculous contrast to behind-the-scenes slapdash, the production on-stage was cool-headed and meticulous. For a company which later proved its prowess and justifiably gained an unparalleled reputation as conveyors of Shakespeare and purveyors of neglected European classics, it's worth noting that their first foray onto the British stage was with this 1675 comedy.

Restoration plays are notoriously deceptive. What seems like a romp is a finely-tuned, subtle critique of the society of the times. It was no coincidence that Donnellan and Ormerod were attracted to this play in 1981, the same year Caryl Churchill's Marlene in *Top Girls* first proclaimed prophetically from the stage of the Royal Court:

'I think the eighties are going to be stupendous [. . .] I think I'm going up up up'.

The Country Wife is full of cynical, sexual manipulation, not least from the protagonist, Horner, who is able to have his way with any woman of his choice, by posing as a eunuch to gull husbands, brothers and lovers. The apparent love these characters are supposed to feel is actually described in a financial parlance, betraying a lust:

'I see all women are like these of the Exchange; who, to enhance the price of their commodities, report to their fond customers offers which were never made 'em' (IIii).

And when the opportunity for canoodling presents itself (most often at a theatre) the love-making is violent:

'He put the tip of his tongue between my lips, and so mousled me — and I said I'd bite it',

says an eager Mrs Pinchwife, so outraging her husband that he threatens to

> 'write whore with this penknife in your face' (IVii).

They're not very nice people. It's hardly genteel comedy. But Cheek by Jowl's production displayed an early delight in the humour of the implicitly grotesque.

Allen Saddler, in his first of many plauditory calls, felt on seeing the production at Plymouth's Arts Centre that one component was particularly rewarding:

> 'I was greatly interested by the pace and technique – and the wardrobe that doubles as an imposing entrance, a cupboard and then tips into a sedan chair: this simple and ingenious prop, designed by Nick Ormerod, deserves an award' (*Guardian* 8/12/81).

One of the telling things about Cheek by Jowl is how its designer, Nick Ormerod, has failed to win any award, despite nominations. British Theatre and its audience is still impressed by large-scale, showy spectacle while paradoxically recognising the wonder of delicate direction which owes so much to simple designs.

While they're a flattering recognition of their pioneering work, awards aren't the *raison d'être* of Cheek by Jowl, though they undoubtedly help their profile in raising funds and audience awareness. Ultimately, it is the people who see the productions who count.

People's views on theatre are demonstrably influenced by a Cheek by Jowl production. Directors glean production ideas; academics are thrown into paroxysms of self-doubt as their deeply held, conservative interpretations of plays are so radically challenged; performers long to attract the attention of a company with whom they would love to work. And Catholic reviewers find exceptions to their rules:

> 'I have always found it hard to laugh at Restoration comedy and to be sorry for any of the highly unpleasant characters who stalk their way through the blood-soaked plots of Restoration tragedy, but *The Country Wife* proved a highly amusing exception' (*The Catholic Herald* 11/9/81).

he style is that of a company which asks us to consider the old piece condescendingly – as a relic . . . It is a critique of the play which they offer rather than the play that Etherege wrote (Eric Shorter *Daily Telegraph* **26/3/86 Donmar Warehouse)**

It is testament to Cheek by Jowl's enthusiasm which never sees them resting on their well-earned laurels, and to their persistent, diverse exploration, that their initial success with a Restoration comedy was not followed up with yet more of the same. In ten years, only one other production has been of a play from this period. It was only after mounting a Shakespeare tragedy, then an adaptation (or new play based upon a novel), another Shakespeare (a romance), a French classic (the last three of which came together at the Donmar Warehouse as an intriguing trilogy), and then their first glorious Shakespeare comedy (the six types of play which distinguish the sections of this book) that Donnellan and Ormerod chose to present their second, and so far latest Restoration play, *The Man of Mode* (joining *A Midsummer Night's Dream* on tour in the Autumn of 1985).

The difficulty of mounting Restoration comedies, is how the play should relate to a contemporary audience, especially when they will probably be expecting a mannered Comedy of Manners. Cheek by Jowl's staging of *The Man of Mode* particularly played on the relationship between play, its past historical context, and its contemporary 1980's audience. It effectively became a play-within-a-play where sneering aristos in full, decadent regalia delivered a disdainful prologue to us standing outside a circular, wooden, low platform. As the play proceeded, within the circular stage, these figures would applaud each others' performances, though glaring at the theatre audience menacingly, tutting, and snapping 'Shh!' sharply, if that audience itself felt induced to applaud. They would groan each time 'the country' was mentioned and generally retain the air of a scoffing, metropolitan arrogance (much of the initial work with characterisation had been with the making of masks, each actor creating features he or she felt would be liberating in rehearsal). 'It was as if these rather wonderful people from 300 years ago had come to perform their play for us and we were bloody lucky to see it,' says Donnellan:

'That enabled them to play it seriously. They were horrified that people should find their emotional extremities funny.

'When we choose plays, we do so because they are great new plays. Those great classic plays are plays about us, intrinsically about who we are. You read a play like *Philoctetes* or *The Man of Mode* and think: "They are about our society". What you don't get in Restoration drama is a sense of class warfare. It's the sexual politics of Restoration comedies that is so fascinating'.

Yet for all its apparent lack of class differentiation, none of the servants appeared in *The Man of Mode*, the company significantly choosing that the periwigged creatures around the stage should condescend to speak their lines. The effect of these heavily made-up observers – white pancake, rouge, yellowing teeth, flouting their flamboyant costumes and long canes with a wily, foxy sneer – was to make the theatre audience treat the play proper as something far more rooted in the present, these alien beings from a historical past (and from a pre-

dictable theatrical tradition) failing to protect their play which they naively supposed to flatter and fawn to them.

Cheek by Jowl's *Man of Mode* was effectively a critique of all the extraneous props with which contemporary productions treat such a play, thus allowing the play proper to be seen afresh with clarity and precision. But the *Daily Telegraph*'s Eric Shorter, unimpressed and unconvinced by the metatheatre of the insulting aristocrats, felt that Etherege had been cheated, his play not given a fair hearing. Martin Hoyle, on the other hand, was delighted that Cheek by Jowl

'give language its due as a means of communication' (*Plays & Players* May 1986 Donmar Warehouse).

As with the controversial presentations of *Twelfth Night* and *The Tempest*, Cheek by Jowl chose to strip away bogus, received assumptions about the play and its performance style, in order to deliver it as they read it. The words, the raw material, were Etherege's. And Cheek by Jowl communicated to the audience what Etherege said and meant to them.

The self-consciousness of social practices in Restoration society is shown in the self-consciousness of the characters: whether assuming French foppery, like the modish man of the play's subtitle, Sir Fopling Flutter; or dazzling turns of phrase, like Dorimant.

Saskia Reeves, who had joined the company to play Hermia in *A Midsummer Night's Dream*, remembers how during that Shakespeare tour, Donnellan was already thinking about the play that he was about to rehearse:

'Declan is a great observer of people and behaviour, watching all the time. He's never still. (Nick's the same, but he's not so energised and obviously electric about it.) When we were playing *The Dream* in Taormina, Sicily, Declan came running in saying: "I've just seen the fop. I've just seen the kind of man who could play the fop". And I said: "Tell me about him" – "Well, he's very camp and he had crisp white shorts on, crisp white socks, crisp white plimsolls, a phoney tan and he was blond". You could just imagine this self-consciously dressed tourist wandering about

Taormina, which is an incredibly self-conscious place. You could see by what Declan had observed in somebody's behaviour how he'd bring out the qualities in that character in that play for an audience. Though *The Man of Mode* was set in period, that quality of the character was there'.

The precision with which the story-telling was staged was symbolised by the two-toned, wooden circular stage, resembling 'a horizontal dartboard' with the cast of ten (doubling of roles being one of Cheek by Jowl's strong characteristics) gathering for the play's prologue 'around the bull's-eye':

'The show is as well-drilled as a piece of clock-work ... another group jerks into speech and motion [suggesting] the operation of a wind-up toy' (Irving Wardle *The Times* 26/3/86 Donmar Warehouse).

Christopher Edwardes, who also saw the Donmar run, gave his analysis of this punctilious control:

'The director has drilled his cast to move from scene to scene as if taking part in a formal dance [...] The effect created as they move with sinister precision from one intrigue to another, is of mechanical creatures caught up in an endless cycle of mindless repetition' (*The Spectator* 5/4/86).

These are precise, if slightly pessimistic responses to the tight style of the production. However, there is something implicit in both appraisals which might frustrate an over-defensive director. That is, that the actors were 'drilled'.

1980's theatre criticism and actors' green-room natter (as in any other decade probably) was dominated by phrases like 'Director's Theatre' spoken with sneering contempt, especially after Simon Callow had his go in a 'Manifesto' at the end of his autobiography *Being an Actor*. The argument goes that actors should not just be the pretty ciphers to strut around the stage at the dictate of the director or the whim of a designer with a grand concept; and they ought to empower themselves to hire and fire the directors.

It's clear that Cheek by Jowl couldn't be accused of 'Designer's Theatre', unless the absence of a huge set on stage was taken as an indication of an austere, holy theatre. However, the charge of 'Director's Theatre' has been made against Donnellan. He eloquently refutes it:

'If the director keeps a very very low profile, then the play will be directed by the writer, the producer, or the most powerful actor. So, there's always a director. You've got to whip up the soufflé so people's ideas mean something; but you don't squash people's ideas with your own. Often when actors are working well, they have no idea what their performance is like. An example of bad acting is looking outside yourself with a third eye. A director is a necessary onlooker.

'We like to think that Cheek by Jowl is an actors' company even though the actors have no political power. (I think it's extremely sad that there aren't any companies of performers who appoint their directors, because there would be nothing more flattering than being appointed by an actors' company to direct. I would see that as an honour.) But Cheek by Jowl is an actors' company because it's about the actors; we always concentrate on them. We are both obsessed by acting and actors. Theatre is the actors' art first and last. Even writing is only part of that artform. Theatre is about the actor and the audience's relationship. So directors and designers come well down the pecking order. Our job is to enable that imaginative fusion to happen, and certainly not just to make an artistic statement of our own'.

The direction of a Cheek by Jowl production is inspired by the actors in the rehearsal room. Where there's comedy, it's executed with a detailed wit not a flaccid slapstick. Whatever the tones of the play, the productions always use a variety of attitudes from the performers to reflect them, and so put the story across clearly to the audience.

When that story involves a cast-list of forty or more, and you're a small-scale company only able to employ a handful of actors, the tale could become fudged and confused, as the actors manically adopt a whirlwind of roles. With *Vanity Fair*, Cheek by Jowl had taken up that challenge.

TELLING TALES

heek by Jowl, with their production
of *Vanity Fair*, gave us an evening which demon-
strated the true magic of theatre at its best. It
wasn't about pretending that painted bits and pie-
es are something different, or that some over-
ated star from another medium is better than he
r she predictably turns out to be in the flesh. This
was about seven particularly talented actors mak-
ng work for their bodies, the space around them,
nd a few deceptively simple accoutrements (*The
Chronicle* 22/12/83 Coleraine Riverside Theatre,
Northern Ireland)

When Donnellan and Ormerod chose to adapt a
nineteenth century novel for the stage, Thackeray's
Vanity Fair, the production owed as much to their
playwriting creativity as it did to the original
nspiration of the novel. And there was a third fac-
or: the actors, who spent ten weeks working on
he adaptation with Ormerod and Donnellan. 'Nick
nd Declan had written this six hour script,'
Amanda Harris, who had joined the company in
982 to play Desdemona in *Othello*, and was now
mbarked on a further eighteen months of wide-
anging theatrical exploration, explains:

'We were all sorts of characters. I was playing old
whores and old ladies all over the place, apart

from my basic character, which was Amelia. W
were sort of guinea pigs: they would try ou
scenes with us, so we very much all joined forces
They have this wonderful streak of brilliance
Declan's wonderful at things that are arch. That'
one of the reasons why *Vanity Fair* worked s
well, because it's a work of archness'.

Vanity Fair was intensely critical of modern ant
social behaviour. After all, vanity is not reserved fo
early nineteenth century characters of fiction. Th
simple, four piece, black, grey and silver set, whic
so delighted *The Chronicle*'s critic (and prompte
some pedantic reviewers to remind us that the co
ours, though little else, were similar, not even th
same, as those used by Theatre Venture's designe
in that company's 1978 production of a differen
stage version of the same novel) was the catalys
for its pointed style of delivery:

> '*More coffee Lord Steyne? said Becky, very la*
> *one night as a party of gentlemen were playin*
> *cards in her snug little drawing-room',*

says Becky, with an interceding, flowing self-narra
tive, appealing in its lightness of touch and warm i
its delivery by Sadie Shimmin, yet curiously unse
tling for audiences. As demonstrated in *The Man o
Mode*, every Cheek by Jowl production has som

kind of audience address effect. Thus the Coleraine critic remarked, 'it wasn't about pretending that painted bits and pieces were something different', the audience never being gulled into thinking that this pretence is for real. ('Show that you are showing', said Brecht to his actors attempting to make his theoretical *verfremdungseffekte* possible in practice.) It's all about telling tales, as Ormerod and Donnellan explain in turn:

'I think we get a lot of dissatisfaction from a lot of theatre which has people walking on stage pretending they've come from somewhere inexplicably off-stage. We strip away that level of deceit. Why pretend this is a real room, or real grass, or a real door, and that you're really walking into a real place? We're saying what is the truth, which is that these are actors who are acting a story. What we're doing is clearing away an accretion of tradition, which has developed post-nineteenth century, of pretence' (Ormerod)

'Another way of putting it is that theatre is lies, complete lies. But theatrical lying is vitally important because it's through that that we can tell each other the truth. Our lives have to be safe, so we go to the theatre to see something dangerous. We assemble in a space and we investigate a fantasy. You use the trappings of lies in order to say something that's truthful, in order that Mrs Bloggs, or whoever, will know what it's like to murder her husband, for instance. We can't experiment with those things in our lives. We're fascinated with the extremities of how people live. We try to tell the truth by means of the lie' (Donnellan).

Movable screens, sporting gutsy Toulouse Lautrec-ish caricatures on one side (in fact the original *Vanity Fair* illustrations) and banquettes on the other, together with a few boxes, were all that were needed to create ballroom, bedroom, and battlefield. The novel is set on the eve of the Battle of Waterloo; and the seven-strong cast – who played over forty parts of both genders, and a couple of growling bloodhounds – sang and played Tchaikovsky's 1812 Overture to evoke the Napoleonic Wars.

Helped by the instantly transforming set – the actors themselves creating a corridor of the Crawley family's portraits, a Ramsgate to Ostend ferry, a church for a wedding – the versatile and agile performers would slip into a role like Glorvina (Andrew Collins) as smoothly as they slipped into the sleeves of the dress held out by two of their fellow actors. The production thus had an unbroken flow of scenes (as in all Cheek by Jowl's productions, there are no awkward breaks in the rhythm, no time to unwrap your sweeties because your attention is wrapped by the play): a 'cinematic fluidity' said Martin Hoyle reviewing the play at the Donmar Warehouse, where it triumphantly finished its eighteen month life on the road with Cheek by Jowl's *Pericles* and *Andromache*. For Hoyle, *Vanity Fair* was 'a visual jigsaw', though the pieces were occasionally ill-fitting:

'There are moments which remind us that such stylisation is a hair's breadth from village hall romps: some of the other travesty parts are perilously close to pantomime dames; but the company's typical virtues of intelligence, vigour and clarity strip the fripperies from what is revealed as a pretty nasty set of grasping egotists' (*Financial Times* 8/1/85).

Duncan Bell – who, along with four others received his Equity card half-way through the tour as Cheek by Jowl were able to afford Equity status – recalls Donnellan and Ormerod's approach to their adaptation:

'We were a group delivering a social history, a myth: something basic to that group of people as a myth is to a tribe. It had both political and personal resonances'.

Some who saw the play at the Donmar Warehouse, like Robert Page from *The Times*, were able to see how the rising bourgeoisie reached a sickening peak in the 1980's, to which Cheek by Jowl were alluding, if only by heavy implication (and to be made more explicit with *A Family Affair* in 1988). Page felt that this was manifest in television escapism, and watched *Vanity Fair* 'like a period *Dallas*' (8/1/85).

Predictably, *Vanity Fair* was received as part of a bandwagon on which the RSC's *Nicholas Nickleby* had ridden. (At the time there was also a stagey, moribund production of *Great Expectations* playing at the Old Vic.) Inevitably some of the techniques (lilting narrative nods to the work's original genre: 'said Mrs Pinkerton', for example) were echoes of that adaptation, and of Mike Alfreds' earlier version of *Bleak House* for Shared Experience. *Nicholas Nickleby*, adapted by David Edgar from Dickens' novel, had re-packaged its packed punch to become a cosy, Christmas, tv treat, sporning the imitative but insubstantial *Les Miserables* (unbelievably from the same RSC team, though significantly ditching Edgar). *Vanity Fair* was a punchy epic, of small-scale physical proportions yet large in its emotional and sociological vistas. *Nicholas Nickleby* had a company of forty. *Vanity Fair* found seven to be ample.

Being a company of seven playing so many roles certainly stretched the actors' contrasting characterisations. Duncan Bell remembers one tired performance where he (the dashing George Osborne) had died just before the interval, caught in the crossfire of the Napoleonic Wars, to return after the break (via a quick cameo as a little boy – George Osborne Jnr., which was confusing enough) as the aged aristocrat, The Marquis of Steyne:

> 'I heard a whisper from the audience: "I thought he'd just died?". So much for convincing versatility!'

Vanity Fair, Cheek by Jowl's third production, was the play which really confirmed their popularity and critical acclaim (this particular adaptation received subsequent productions, including one by drama students at the Royal Scottish Academy of Dramatic Art in 1985, at the Guildhall School of Music and Drama in 1990, and a professional production off-off-Broadway in 1991). Within eighteen months, the *Vanity Fair* which had received a *Scotsman* Fringe First at Edinburgh's 1983 August Fringe Festival, was playing at London's Donmar Warehouse and had been nominated, along with *Pericles* and *Andromache*, for the Society of West End Theatre's Olivier Award for 'Most Promising Newcomer', which the company duly received at the 1985 gala. Entertaining, approved, promising – Cheek by Jowl had earned its laurels by presenting a quasi-documentary of human greed, wealth and corruption in a mind-boggling spectacle. It was the type of magic in the art of telling tales that was to prove an essential part of their work.

he writing so closely reflects his directorial style – vivid, emotional and dramatically daring. It seems we are witnessing the birth of the rare beast: a writer who pens theatre, not words (Andy Lavender *City Limits* 23/11/89)

Declan Donnellan can spin a good yarn. The phrasing, the choice of vocabulary, the moments of incredulous tremor in the voice, the confidence of the challenging statements – he's a fine craftsman. His face lights up, he gracefully gesticulates, and you're compelled to laugh at his effusive humour before he's even reached the climax (and there are usually three or four deliberately false peaks along the way). He can pull the face of a Great British Bulldog, distorted, grotesque, but tough; his cheeks can look like a chubby cherub's, flushing with coy innocence; his nostrils can flare with the feigned arrogance of a barrister; his brow can furrow while deviously wrestling with the chopped logic of a lapsed Irish Catholic – and you really ought to see him at full fettle with his natural comic foil, Nick Ormerod. Donnellan's is an absorbing physical performance; and yet you find yourself gripped by the detail and the main thrust of the spoken tale. With Donnellan, actions can only speak as loud as the words.

This enthusiasm and relish which Donnellan displays as a raconteur, and with which you find your own imagination irresistibly whirring, transforms itself into a sophisticated discipline when he directs a play. Given the opportunity to write that play, Donnellan excels. You know that the story will come first, necessitating a vibrant context. It's the way he tells 'em.

Donnellan and Ormerod instinctively knew that the tale of Lady Betty, the Hangwoman of Roscommon, would make a wonderful piece of theatre. It's a turn of the nineteenth century story, partly true, partly myth. It's well-known in West Ireland's Roscommon, where Donnellan lived as a young child in his parents' pub (on the rehearsal-room noticeboard were pictures of his own family). It's also a history recorded in the 1850's from eye-witness accounts and a collective folk-memory by Sir William Wilde, Oscar's father.

For various reasons, playwrights approached felt unable to see through a commission on this occasion. So, on purloined hotel writing paper, as he travelled on the international tour of *The Tempest* and *Philoctetes*, Donnellan spent six months between Oslo and Bucharest preparing a rehearsal draft himself. He was fortunate in having space to explore the story through preliminary workshops at the National Theatre's Studio with performers who weren't part of the actual cast: including Mark Addy, Toby Byrne, Rachel Joyce and Clive Rowe.

A personal Irish culture and tradition, and its public theatrical expressions and forms, were apparent in both play and production. From the outset, the words reveal a flinty poetry, demanding that they be matched by a gritty exposition. At the very opening of the play, Betty challenges a singing and dancing Chorus: 'Have you told them who I am?'. And then she implores them to:

> 'Cut my image in the air. [. . .] Etch my features in their hearts. [. . .] And is that all? Is that all me now? Broken words? Flesh it for them. Pump it with blood the way I was young. Dance my story in the dirt. Harder, harder . . .' (Prologue)

and the company oblige, as they take us through the rough patchwork and fine tapestry of the tactile story of a woman who, condemned to hang for unwittingly murdering her own son 'because she had no money and was starving', is reprieved as the hangman runs away, becoming the hangwoman herself, employed by the English.

The play demands a sensual production. There were thumping jigs of threatening exuberance (both 'subversive and so like the drilled, perpetual rhythm of oppressed Irish life' – Michael Ratcliffe *Observer* 12/11/89, on tour); and real dancing competitions on stage, unremitting challenges between two performers every night in dazzling turns of nifty footwork which were always spontaneous, never

choreographed – between Ray McBride, a former World Champion Irish Step Dancer, and Lawrence Evans, an English Junior Irish Dancing Champion (the nine-year-old Donnellan himself won first prize for dancing the Jig at Roscommon Fair).

There was an eeriness in the personifications of Night and Silence, who haunt Betty as provocative alter egos; yet a gutsy earthiness from Cold – Phil McKee pouring a basin of icy water over his head and bare torso – and Morning – Lucy Tregear, bare-chested, blond-haired, and starkly spotlit in Ben Ormerod's (no relation) sometimes soft, sometimes brutal lighting design.

Jane Gibson – who joined Cheek by Jowl as Movement Director for the first time on *Lady Betty*, after her successful relationship with Donnellan, Ormerod and Paddy Cunneen at the National Theatre with *Fuente Ovejuna* – describes how her skills blended into the approach of the whole production:

'We worked on basic Irish steps and techniques every day with the company. Declan made the space for it – not to be nice to anyone, but because he intelligently realised that he could work with it, and it was going to bear fruit. He never rushed anything. The movement became implanted in their bodies. It wasn't just dancing to music, because it was exploring the characters of Silence and Cold too. How should they move? It was thus important to have the movement and the music right there from the beginning. It's hopeless when it's just stuck on at the end'.

There was real smell in this production too. Betty sketches – she is a keen-eyed observer – and is asked to 'draw us up the smell of a pair of sausages spitting in the pan', the 'spitting' alone making an imagined whiff of cooking sausage-fat pass our hungry nostrils. We smelled the peat as it burned in the braziers; and the pipe tobacco smoke from a previous scene left an uncanny odour for the description of the 'sweet smell of death' in Roscommon Gaol.

All this wasn't just for atmospheric effect. The risible Irish character under the occupation of the morally enfeebled English was starkly presented: Ormerod's set of nooses hanging from the ceiling, the gallows made of rough hewn branches, which also represented house frames; the zest of Paddy Cunneen's ballads and original music played by the company on an impressive array of fiddles, drums and bodrhans; Gibson's wild Irish reels – all contrasted with the implacability of the English overlords. When the play ran at Islington's Almeida, it was set against that theatre's impressively imposing back brick wall, Roscommon Gaol itself by suggestion, a grim monument of English occupation and a gutless facade of severity and authority.

Sally Dexter (Lady Betty) jokes that the play felt constantly alive throughout the run because she could never get the lines right since they were always being adjusted on the British tour (*Lady Betty* was never seen abroad). She makes the more fundamental observation that, as an actress,

'if you ever felt you'd finished it, how could you possibly go back and do it the next night? Of course, you had to have a certain amount of structure; but the structure was freeing and gave you an onward feeling'.

The musical composition for *Lady Betty* is recognised by Cunneen as being

'a really powerful way of not just setting the scenes, but, quite apart from suggesting the musical life of Ireland, enhancing things like the crowds. We put people up on the barricades and had them playing crowd noises on their violins and clarinets. There is a space for music and sound to contribute something concrete. We can play the role that a big expensive set, a swish costume, or a large company of actors might play. The music has a function'.

A few, like *City Limits'* Lyn Gardner did feel that:

'Politics are sacrificed to the picturesque [. . .] and the result is rather too cosy to serve as any comment on English imperialism and Irish ignorance' (6/12/89 Almeida).

There certainly was a warm appeal about much of the production, and it might have occasionally blocked out the harshness of the plot, or the terror imposed upon the Irish by the English. Just in case we were ever to feel too cosy, the green-jacketed Ray McBride as O'Leary, the Gaol's turnkey and black-humoured profiteer, would knock us out of any comfort by deliberately drawing attention to our patronising, leprechaunish identification of the charming Irish. He constantly stepped out of the play, saying:

> 'Jesus, Mary and Joseph. [. . .] Isn't it a terrible thing to fight your way to the theatre of a night and have to put up with the likes of this. All this suffering and screaming. And sure you all trying to hold down your little jobs, and hoping to catch the last bus home, and coming to the theatre in the hope of a little cheer to get yez through the rest of your miserable week and what do you get but grunting and groaning. I can hear yez all saying "O'Leary" [. . .] will you entertain us in the name of all that's holy and give us a little ember to light us through the dark of our working lives. And O'Leary will oblige. [. . .] Here now is a jolly little song from O'Leary to give yez a secret smile as yez lean over yer word processors tomorrow.
>
> (SINGS) "Have you ever seen an Irishman wear
> a funny hat?
>
> Have you ever seen an Irishman go rat-tat-tat?
>
> Have you ever seen an Irishman fall down flat?
>
> No! You've never seen an Irishman do anything
> like that.
>
> De deedle de deedle de deedle dee dee."
>
> How's that for the crack? And nothing political in it as God is my witness' (O'Leary's Song).

At face value, it is a reassuring interlude. It is a basic theatrical device supposedly to knock us out of any complacency, or disappointment we might feel, were we unsophisticated theatre-goers. But it's much more than this. It had a similar effect as Anne White's effing and blinding Porter in Cheek by Jowl's *Macbeth* had – a shocking insistence that we must never be gulled into thinking that theatre is for real. And in fulfilling the silly expectation of a predominantly English audience, about the chirpiness of our self-imposed Irish archetypes, it can be unsettling.

Clearly, a point about theatre's artifice is not the only one being made. Both specifically at this point, and through the plot and characterisations as a whole, Donnellan is playing upon the tension of an English, Protestant power within an Irish, Catholic community – in short, the history of Ireland is being performed before our eyes. By lulling us into a cosy picturesqueness, Donnellan has made us aware of the condescension with which we can treat the Emerald Isle. And then we have to examine the attitudes portrayed in the story:

'This is not just a picturesque folk-tale. Donnellan shows how the Irish blarney and superstition conceals a streetwise pragmatism, counterpointing it against the bluff moral superiority and hypocrisy of the English rulers' (Mark Cook *Hampstead & Highgate Gazette* 15/12/89 Almeida).

The folk-tale is picturesque to offset the irony of that context. Soft Irish voices exchanging genial repartee sounds nice. That they do it by the side of a glowing fire probably looks lovely. But the tableau exists because the people are hungry, cold, and living in dire poverty.

Lady Betty was a celebration filled with sadness, a vivacious theatrical treat in dangerous conflict with a story fuelled by political horror, personal terror and a humanity made up of flawed individuals. As a new play, *Lady Betty* is not perhaps the style of drama you would expect from the pen of contemporary playwrights from a Royal Court stable. But *Lady Betty* has left its mark, imprinted in the memory of a theatre-going public as an event of indivisible parts – a whole experience.

SUMMATE CLASSICS

ANDROMACHE & THE CID

he startling assumption of both productions was that their authors were writing about human beings. Instead of stately parades of bewigged puppets, there were companies in modern dress. Instead of verse delivered on stilts, there was idiomatic speech. And instead of idealised moral anguish, there were actual questions of moral choice. Declan Donnellan and his team pay their authors the rare compliment of expecting them to make sense (Irving Wardle *The Times* 14/2/87)

Though *Lady Betty* is Cheek by Jowl's only production of a new play so far (ignoring the early Low Countries' tour of the *Gotcha/Rack Abbey* double-bill and the novel adaptation of *Vanity Fair*), new writing is not something that has been ignored. Donnellan and Ormerod are constantly reading new plays by British playwrights. But they have found their imaginations stirred far more profoundly by foreign classics (when taking a break from Shakespeare). It is not an easy sentimentalism which attracts Cheek by Jowl; it is a wide-ranging physical and emotional panorama, combining dark drama with light theatre, which naturally draws the company to such plays.

That virtually all of the European plays chosen by Cheek by Jowl have never been seen in Britain before – sometimes an oversight of nearly four hundred years – doesn't make those plays mere novelties, historical curios for the avid theatre-watcher in pursuit of first-night sightings. Of course, Cheek by Jowl along with a number of other companies are providing a kind of service to a culturally-starved British theatre-going public; but they are also celebrating a drama, and inviting the audience to share in the creation of that celebration, through a theatrical panache ignited from the spark which those texts fire.

To some this might seem to be a decadent, art-for-art's-sake exercise. Max Stafford-Clark, in his fascinating account of his rehearsals of *The Recruiting Officer* and *Our Country's Good* for the Royal Court, *Letters to George*, describes his view of 1980's London theatre to the eighteenth century playwright, George Farquhar:

'How far should the Theatre Manager move to accommodate the taste of the town? Obviously, compromise is a dirty word, but we all swim in the same pool, and it takes a seer or a fool to defy the tide of popular opinion more than once in a season. [. . .] London's current tide in theatrical chic is swinging towards groups such as Théâtre de Complicité (enormously skilled absurdism) and to Cheek by Jowl (cheeky revivals of the classics). It's veering towards entertainment rather than to provocative debate. Plays that take on public issues may no longer carry the public with them. [. . .] The voice of theatre becomes more important. Its values in illuminating different corners of society and in explaining ourselves to ourselves has never been needed more'.

Plays from the past, especially in a so-called 'cheeky' revival, do indeed provoke debate and tell us masses about ourselves. Joyous revivals of classic plays won't necessarily indulge audiences in glib entertainment. Through a purposeful pleasure, calling upon deep emotional reserves, an enlivening enquiry and a nudging (rather than hectoring) provocation, we can indeed learn much by drawing

on a collective contemporary psyche, as well as recognising that which we have inherited. This was precisely what was so effective about Stafford-Clark's own revival of *The Recruiting Officer*, though probably because it was presented in tandem with *Our Country's Good*, Timberlake Wertenbaker's strong adaptation of Thomas Keneally's 1987 novel *The Playmaker*, charting 18th century British convicts' discovery of themselves through a production of *The Recruiting Officer* on arrival in Australia – 'explaining ourselves to ourselves' through a closely scrutinised, multi-layered, cultural and sociological history.

Foreign classics unseen in this country are obviously new to virtually everyone, and definitely new in English on British stages. With the presentation of foreign work, obviously a translation has to be found that is stageable. Cheek by Jowl usually commission new translations from living writers (*Sara* and *The Doctor of Honour* being the exceptions). The work is not 'new writing' in its strictest sense. But it is new, raw, and most importantly treated as such, rather than as a sacrosanct museum piece, when Cheek by Jowl tackle it.

The first two British premières of foreign plays presented by Cheek by Jowl were two pillars of seventeenth century French classicism: from Racine in the 1660's (*Andromache*, given its British professional première in 1984) and Corneille in the 1630's (*The Cid*, half-known as a film of epic proportions, but unknown on the stage in this country until 1986). This important strand of Cheek by Jowl's work materialised as an inevitable development of their work.

Their range of plays is that of a visionary young company hungry to develop an exploratory repertoire, willing to try anything. Cheek by Jowl were evolving rapidly with their company of actors; Donnellan and Ormerod were growing in confidence as well as know-how. Amanda Harris, playing in the four productions from *Othello* to *Andromache* describes the development in terms of what Donnellan and Ormerod saw that the actors needed in rehearsal to excite their imaginations:

'With *Othello*, we pretty much got down to it. With *Vanity Fair*, we had a long ten week rehearsal period, improvising and trying things out. With *Pericles*, we had a movement and voice person, so we started to do more thorough exercises. Each process for each play became more sophisticated in terms of how we would start rehearsals every morning. By the time *Andromache* came along, we had an Alexander Technique teacher as well. Each course of action taken by Nick and Declan was appropriate to the play we were working on, to bring out the best in it. So Alexander was right for *Andromache* because of the stillness that that play required. The first time we did it we felt ten foot tall, and by feeling that, it helped convey the sense of power'.

The physical poise was apparent in the considered production. Not every Cheek by Jowl show is cheerfully anarchic, contrary to a popular impression. *Andromache* and *The Cid* were calm, yet passionate, as the mood took them.

Andromache joined the repertoire as Cheek by Jowl became more ambitious during their long tour of *Vanity Fair* and *Pericles*. It gave the performers a chance to play at something different again.

In discovering neglected classics, Cheek by Jowl have been called 'inexhaustible dramatic ferrets' (Georgina Brown *Independent* 27/4/89). But Donnellan, while flattered, is wary of such praise:

'The most frightening thing about analysing what you've done in retrospect is that you give it an intellectual, and consequently very scary gloss. When we're asked what was our intention after the event, we can come up with a million grand statements about what we wanted to do. For instance, we never wanted to première European classics: we just liked *Andromache*, thought it went well, and then learnt about *The Cid*. Afterwards we look back and say what others tell us, which is that we pioneer European classics. But it makes it sound as though it was all rather clever and premeditated, which it wasn't'.

So, rather than championing a cause to make foreign classics accessible at this stage of their development – though this was the outcome of what did become a pioneering force for a European voice in British theatre – Cheek by Jowl arrived at *Andromache* in response to various needs and potentials from within the company. It was a fortuitous pragmatism of Cheek by Jowl's instincts,

upon which they have continued to capitalise.

As a supposed exposition of the French classical ideal, it's significant that none of the characters in *The Cid* and *Andromache* manage to live up to their 'name', failing to be honourable, subject to the gory aspects of their glory. In *The Cid*, the Infanta modestly states:

'I would rather

Take my own life than stoop below my rank' (Iii)
and Don Diego humbly suggests to Rodrigo:

'A man who can live

Without honour does not deserve to live' (Iiii).

What attracts Donnellan and Ormerod to such plays are the characters, who aren't perfect angels, but corrupted humans, incorrigibly striving for an ideal and thus making their failure all the more painful. They're too proud to say what they really think or want, until it's too late:

'Should an enraged mistress be taken at her word!

Couldn't you have seen what I was really thinking?

*Couldn't you tell from my outbursts that what
my tongue*

*Uttered was constantly belied by my true feel-
ings' (Viii),*

Hermione exclaims to Orestes whose henchmen
have just murdered Pyrrhus (*Andromache*). The
ironies are positive, not pessimistic, for they
celebrate our inconstancy and inconsistencies,
bringing out the monster in us all. How dull to be
perfect. How perfectly exciting to be flawed. And
the very extremes of what the characters go
through – all obsessed with one passion each,
swinging between the distant poles of love and
hate with unrelenting frequency, even to the point
of death – are what make them appealing:

'The fear of seeing what you most desire refused'
(Andromache *IIIvi).*

The very style of the translations of these classic
works, often chatty ('Well what's keeping him then'
– *Andromache*), illustrate the wider aspects of the
themes of the productions. The limits and confines
of the strict form of the alexandrines have been
broken, freeing the words in idiomatic diction,
transposing the time in the productions into our
own century. The costumes weren't strictly modern
dress, since *Andromache* and *The Cid* never made it
beyond the 1940's. *Andromache* alone caused confusion amongst commentators who couldn't agree
on the decade in which it was set. *The Guardian*
thought the time was the 1930's; the *Kentish
Gazette* the 1940's; *The Financial Times* the 1950's;
The Observer hedged its bets, plumping for the late
forties and early fifties; and *Time Out* was even
more hesitant, committing itself only to an early
twentieth century aristocratic milieu. Whatever the
time ('it was very specifically the post War year of
1948, to correspond to the post Trojan War setting,'
says Ormerod) Racine plays with his own time warp
between the late seventeenth century in which he
lived, and Ancient Greece from where his story
comes.

Because the spoken word was conversational, it
meant that the audience could get at the story,
destroying any anticipation of preciousness, jostling
the classicism with contemporary theatre. Cheek by
Jowl aren't Vandals, smashing up the text with the
German predilection for *klassischezertrummerung*

which throws classics up in the air to see how the
pieces fall. Cheek by Jowl seeks fidelity to the play
while being conscious that it isn't being presented
in a cultural vacuum. The productions may seem
mock-heroic, satirising the values that the
playwrights might have held dear. But Cheek by
Jowl is interested in the absurdities of what the
characters put themselves through.

The success of their two French plays, and the
spur for subsequent recreations of European classics, may not seem extraordinary as Britain sheds
its cultural insularity in the 1990's. But such plays,
and their startling productions, were rare even in
the mid eighties. Cultural xenophobia is nothing
new to Britain. For centuries we have arrogantly
assumed our culture to be the best in the world and
scorned the need for the culture of Europe or that
from further afield (while assuming, of course, that
they always needed us). Even in 1989, A. L. Senter
found one artistic director of a major British company having doubts over the impact of foreign
infiltrators:

'Terry Hands, Keeper of the Flame as Director of
the RSC, is thoroughly sceptical. "I tend to think
that a lot of nonsense is talked about the
European Classics. A lot of the plays are like the
wine which tastes like nectar on a Greek beach
only to resemble vinegar when you open a bottle
at home" ' (*Evening Standard* 16/3/89).

While that may be the general impression, it's
thanks to a whole host of companies like Cheek by
Jowl that this assertion, implying there's nothing
like a Great British Pint, has been at least partially
disproved in the particular. Our thirst for European
classics has become even greater since the productions of those plays have been so good.

Andromache's style of presentation was refreshing. Confidantes carried neat handbags, not
because they were the reputation-bashing side-
kicks they can so often descend into, but because
that is what the society depicted expected from
them. They became ironic commentators, critics of
their so-called betters. And the voice of the powerless was, as so consistently with Cheek by Jowl,
given vent as they showed their malaise with the
suffering of their masters and mistresses, wiping
away their tears with a tissue, not out of concern,

but as a tiresome aspect of their role as State functionaries – with much yawning and clock-watching to hammer the point home. 'You're working yourself up over nothing,' Cleonie reproaches her mistress Hermione about Orestes (IIi) (and it's Orestes to whom Hermione then says: 'Oh dear, dismal as always' (IIii), all the characters effectively recognising their own high-flown outrage with self-inflicted bathos).

Though the verse form had been freed by the translator, David Bryer, Donnellan and Ormerod's staging was not to lose the restriction of the play's themes:

'Naval uniformed princes and black-suited widows prowl the set's circumference like caged animals pacing out the inexorable constrictions of their destiny' (Martin Hoyle *Financial Times* 10/8/84 Pavillion Gardens' Paxton Suite, Buxton Festival British première).

Michael Coveney, reviewing his first Cheek by Jowl production, and with the Glasgow Citizens' work very much in his mind, didn't like the ironic Englishness of the production, finding it trivial and belittling:

'The problems of rhetoric and staging are ducked, rolled into a cosily convenient Fringe package with safety the norm and risk at a premium' (*Financial Times* 25/1/85 Donmar Warehouse).

The emotions were indeed expressed frankly:

'Where am I? What have I done?
What should I do now?
Why am I so excited . . . yet so miserable?
I run around in circles within this palace –
If only I could know if it's love or hate I feel!'
(Hermione *Andromache* Vi).

Where Ormerod had given *Andromache* a black-and-white zodiacal floor to reflect that it might be the will of nature or the fate of the gods that predestined the people of the play, *The Cid* had a complicated mosaic floor, a maze of interweaving patterns of human passion and artifice. *The Cid* was firmly set in early 1930's Spain, just before the Civil War. Corneille's dominant themes throughout his tragedies of love versus duty, private feeling in conflict with public emotions, were exquisitely staged. The code of conduct within this environment may have belittled 'great issues of state' to 'a game of cat and mouse' (Francoise Delas-Reisz *Times Educational Supplement* 30/1/87 Donmar Warehouse) but that was, perhaps, the idea. These were living people, coping with the strictures of the codes of honour which informed a way of life. In casting those values in an ironic shadow, Cheek by Jowl's production might have mocked the past, but it also drew attention to the humbug of today's mock-heroic.

Quick black-outs, a few guitar chords with a Hispanic stamp of the feet and clap of the hands, punctuated the scenes, enhancing the imposing atmosphere. It wasn't a pleasant tale – the *Watford & West Herts Review* headlined their report on the production 'CID VICIOUS' (16/10/86).

If this austere production of *The Cid*, compelling in its intimacy, confirmed 'Cheek by Jowl as the current brand-leaders in the British Anti-Rhetoric School' (Michael Ratcliffe *Observer* 21/9/86 Kings Lynn Fermoy Centre), then their next European classic in 1988 was to show them at their scurrilous best, with an anti-rhetoric taken to the extreme by the vernacular nitty-gritty of one playwright poking his nose into the dirt of another.

s the rise and rise of the obnoxious ones rolls inexorably on, you become aware, if you care for this kind of theatre and this kind of politics, that you are watching not just a production but an event; crowned as it is by a remarkable ending which truly leaves the greed and hypocrisies of this age pinned down for all to see (**Andy Lavender** *City Limits* **5/5/88 Donmar Warehouse**)

By 1988, Thatcherism was at its peak. A third election victory in June 1987 had secured an apparently unassailable iron fortress for the Iron Lady. And Enterprise Culture was all the rage.

Social and economic duress, where an aspiring bourgeoisie would stop at nothing to gain the upper hand, wasn't new. It merely reached an ugly climax, justified by a shallow political philosophy. Cheek by Jowl's two Restoration play productions had already drawn contemporary parallels with the world of Restoration drama, highlighting that period's seedy social phenomena inviting us to recognise the implications for 1980's society. But it was not until *A Family Affair* that they were to attack the very artless heart of Thatcherite

attitudes. And, as *City Limits'* Andy Lavender appreciated, it was not through some barking on the left (the Royal Court's production of Caryl Churchill's *Serious Money* had transferred to the West End's Wyndhams Theatre in July 1987, to the delight of yuppie city slickers who kept that show running for ten months) but by a joyous celebration of the art of theatre itself. Those whose pleasure was renewed in this type of thrilling theatre had a boost to their radical, critical and satirical politics which had been wallowing in jaded apathy and depressed impotence.

Donnellan and Ormerod had seen Ostrovsky's play performed in Finland (where they have mounted guest productions of *Macbeth* and *Philoctetes* for the Finnish National Theatre, both in anticipation of Cheek by Jowl's productions). Convinced of its theatrical potential and timely critique in Britain, they commissioned a translation from the London University academic, David Budgeon, which was meticulously faithful to the original, but evidently unsatisfactory for the stage, being tied up in the specific Moscow bureaucratic details of the 1850's on the page. About to cast the play, they rapidly looked around for an adaptor to approach this text with the same appropriate literary disrespect with which Cheek by Jowl always respects its theatrical realisations.

This is not a disregard for the perceived spirit of the original writing. But nor is it a distorting of a play through interpretation, as Donnellan explains:

'It's dangerous to talk to us about our choices as we fall into the trap of talking about it intellectually, when we would very rarely discuss the play intellectually in the rehearsal process. We might have an emotional discussion about the play, to try and find its emotional truth. (The centre of our rehearsals and our approach is far more emotional than it sometimes appears.) As we've matured, we're more confident in relying on the emotional strength of the play rather than making it make clever points about us now.

'But any work of art changes the participants to the act. Not necessarily by the indoctrination of an intellectual belief but by presenting a fresh and fascinating universe, which invites us to reconsider how we connect to our own world.

'It's very important that the director and the designer don't do the audience's job for them. It's very important that you don't keep them out of the relationship with the actor. The audience will respond emotionally and then deal with that. It's for the audience to interpret, not for us'.

Through a source at the Royal Court, the playwright Nick Dear was suggested for the adaptation, whose *Art of Success* for the RSC in 1986 had attacked a prevalent mood in an eighteenth century London with clear and explicit anachronistic references to our own times. Through the intellectual, political and artistic battle of Hogarth, Fielding and Walpole, Dear created a world in which censorship and compromise ruled the day.

Dear was quick to recognise Donnellan and Ormerod's initial attraction to *A Family Affair*'s story and its resonances. There were things in the Ostrovsky original which clearly had applications for 1988; and it was these which Dear skilfully made apparent. 'The original plot in the Russian had much more financial machinations going on', he explains,

'much more wheeler-dealer scams which eventu-

ally got boring. You didn't need to know the detail of it as they did in the 1850's and 1860's. For them, it was a very new idea that people were on the fiddle in a massive way. (It wasn't new in society, but it hadn't really been exposed in Russian drama before.) For us, it's not such a big deal; we take it for granted. So it didn't seem necessary to go down all the little by-roads of that plot. We had to try and reduce the plot to something which supported the play and also made sense'.

Dear had received a telephone call from his agent one November afternoon in Manchester, where he was Writer in Residence at the Royal Exchange Theatre. He was told that Cheek by Jowl was sounding him out about potential involvement in the project. Intrigued, because he had never adapted before and didn't have a single word of Russian, except 'vodka', he jumped on an Intercity 125 down to London to see Cheek by Jowl's acclaimed *Macbeth*, which was nearing the end of its Donmar Warehouse run. Impressed, and with a copy of the Budgeon translation thrust into his hand by Ormerod and Donnellan, he returned to his

Manchester attic to write a first draft in a staggering two and a half weeks on his newly-purchased Amstrad word-processor.

This speed of the first draft's formation shouldn't make us forget the extensive work in which Dear and the company regularly engaged, in rehearsal and on the tour, constantly re-focusing the new script's sharp writing. (Donnellan apparently suggested that Ostrovsky's script gave the impression that it had only taken a fortnight to compose anyway . . . .) Directors of new plays are nearly always in the privileged position of having the writer in attendance at rehearsal. The translator or adaptor of a dead writer's work is the next best thing. Dear actually takes a principled position about being in on the rehearsals of his work (there are some frightened directors, and some arrogant ones, who feel creatively stifled, or irritated, by the presence of the playwright). Once there, all reap the benefits. When the play's complexities are being unknotted by the company, it cuts short a lot of ponderous dwelling on irrelevant layers if the source of the material is on hand to explain. With any new work, suggestions and reactions from the company affect and influence the writer's fine-tuning. The actress, Lesley Sharp, expands:

'It wasn't a Joint Stock experience in terms of improvising scenes and then asking the playwright to go away and write it up. It was a new play, and having done a lot of new work I think it's brilliant if writers are in the rehearsal room, because you have access to the person whose imagination put it down on the page. We weren't subverting the material; but if there was an idea in rehearsal that could be hitched up by the writing, Nick was keen to do that and encouraged it'.

Dear actually had until mid-January to complete the first draft, but he'd promised himself a Christmas holiday. Adrenalin flowing – with the frantic, disciplined pace (that significantly never allowed time for self-consciousness) which informed the writing and the subsequent production – he created a pared-down but vicious version, emulating Ostrovsky's acidic wit, but bringing his own distinctive voice to swipe at a Thatcherite mentality.

Yelling from the stage is not the subtlest of ways to shift audience's opinions. If anything, it makes them switch off from what are no doubt heartfelt resentments about a morally corrupt *status quo*. *A Family Affair* avoided this by some startling audience manipulation. It was bold, but never crass; entertaining but never vulgar; leftwards-leaning in exposing the get-rich-quick mentality, but not dogmatic propaganda. Perhaps there's a hidden purpose in this – to shift the audience's moral and political position by shifting their sensibilities?

At the end of Ostrovsky's play, three of the characters (the solicitor Rispolozhensky, the scheme-merchant Lazar, and the servant Tishka) temporarily break out of character to address the audience and ask for their moral support. Dear recognises that this is the shock-tactics of a playwright cramming all his theatrical ambitions into his first play. There is a spirit of adventurousness which is ultimately what makes it attractive. It's not the form – apart from the mechanism at the end it is a highly conventional, four-act, sitting-room drama, with four male and four female characters, each representing various layers of the social strata – but the subject and its treatment which is very risqué. Ostrovsky lost his job as clerk to the court because the shady business on stage exposed, through the character of the solicitor Rispolozhensky, the involvement of the legal profession. This was a play that wasn't actually performed but banned before it reached the stage by Tsar Nicholas I. The play received a number of successful readings throughout the 1850's and was eventually allowed to be publicly produced in Tsar Alexander II's reign, with a ninth character introduced: an arresting officer arriving at the end of the play to banish all the characters to gaol.

Dear's not one to drop a good and exciting idea, always prepared to develop a naive impetus into a sophisticated, multi-layered event where the form reflects the content, the content dictates the form. Encouraged by Donnellan, he extended Ostrovsky's crude mechanism and ambience and had the whole cast re-emerging into the auditorium at the play's climax, with the houselights brought up, to accuse Lazar of wilful neglect and wrong-doings towards them (a vain hypocrisy, since they were complaining at being dropped from his money-making plans). The convention of apologies and asides is already established in the play, and Dear merely took this to an extreme conclusion – like the actors in a Cheek by Jowl production, the writers too are invited by Donnellan to push to the extremities of their craft and imagination. In the middle of this appeal, Lazar nastily uses the audience's new-found attention to advertise his new department store: 'You'll all be hugely welcome. Quality goods. Incredible value for money'. But there is also a deliberate confusing of the audience's response (similar to the reaction to O'Leary in *Lady Betty*) when Lipochka, Lazar's new wife, shrieks at the cast to get back on stage:

> 'Get back here and sing the song like you're sup-posed to! It's the end of the play! These good people don't go to the theatre to hear a lot of political nonsense. It's not fashionable any more'.

The company reluctantly comply, and Lazar and Lipochka triumphantly proclaim: 'Now that's what we call . . . family entertainment!'.

It is a send-up of audience expectations, and a back-handed comment on the contemporary theatrical and cultural scene in Britain. The scrutiny of cultural politics is facilitated by the theatricality.

This is important to recognise in Cheek by Jowl's work. To use theatre as a provocative, political medium, you first have to reclaim theatre. If Cheek by Jowl have been reluctant to mount contemporary plays whose politics are worn on a well-worn sleeve, then they have greatly contributed to the resuscitation of the stage as a magnificent medium of extraordinary possibilities. New writers are beginning to embrace that potential. Reinvesting theatricality back into drama can only improve the delivery, and writing, of new plays with political themes.

A Family Affair is in fact riddled with political attacks. The plot itself – of a daughter in cahoots with her new husband (former assistant to her father, the boss) to move up the social ladder (a posher house and the latest French fashions – gaudy, pink, frilly dresses) by a clever scam whereby dad pronounces himself bankrupt, is gulled into handing over his business interests to his new son-in-law, who rejects him, quite happy for

dad to languish in a debtor's jail – bears all the hallmarks of a 1980's scandal. Contained within that, there are frequent references to the aspiring petit-bourgeoisie: both in the observations that other characters make of each other, and the way they condemn themselves out of their own mouths. Lipochka (all the grotesque anxiety of a spoiled child in Lesley Sharp's Olivier Award-nominated, comedy performance) changes her opinion of her upbringing to suit herself:

> 'You didn't teach me everything I know. Proper people did. The truth is, mama, you never got educated at all. You don't know a single thing. And when I popped out of you, what was I fit for? I hadn't the first idea about life. I behaved like a child. I couldn't dance. I didn't know what cutlery to use for the fish course. I was a completely pointless being. But when I got out on my own, I took a look around at the world of taste and sensibility, and I improved myself. And now I have to accept that I'm vastly better equipped for life than most people' (Act I).

Yet later:

> 'Oh, these stupid peasants! What have they done? They brought me up nicely, gave me a decent education, introduced me to all the finer things in life, and now the idiots have gone and bankrupted themselves' (Act III).

Dear's is a brilliant critique of the snobbery and snideness of these petit-bourgeois monsters, the nouveau gentry lambasting the humbug regentrification of their social competitors. Ustinya – the matchmaker, all petty pretensions from Marcia Warren – has nothing but contempt for a family which she is happy to exploit in return for a sable coat to be catwalked along the High Street:

> 'Their mouths will hang open and they'll dribble. They'll envy me so much their noses will drop off',

she exclaims with a crude, violent glee.

Dear humorously captures the diction of his characters. The mother, Agrafena (Anne White), not comprehending the financial state of the family business (even if she did, she'd behave in the same way to keep up appearances) is always keen to be ostentatiously 'generous' as a way of showing off the family's social success. 'We don't stint in this house', she says about holding a 'soirée at our gaff', the jarring of French politesse and crass slang a summation of her character:

> Agrafena: I don't want these tasty snacks to go to waste. Everybody come and eat some. Ustinya, will you take a tiny weeny vodka?
>
> Ustinya: Yes, please. The best people always take a glass at this hour, you know.
>
> Agrafena: Do they? Samson Bolshov, move your behind, so we can get at the scoff (Act III).

'In respectable people's homes the atmosphere's a bit more relaxed, like they're not trying to prove nothing,' says Tishka (Paul Stacey). The double negative here is probably intentional, for 'respectable' no doubt means the opposite of what it seems to say, a code for self-promoting respectability. Though Tishka is a servant, he's not a character to whom we should attach any moral superiority. He merely offers a different perspective on the dominant sentiment of the play, still revealing the mercantile spirit of gambling, stealing, accumulating and greed which permeates this society.

There is also a ripeness of language, which obviously offended some:

'Nick Dear's lively adaptation was brought right up to date, and included plenty of bad language which shocked some in the audience' (Bury Free Press 15/4/88 Theatre Royal Bury St. Edmunds).

But it wasn't just the swearing which may have been upsetting. The style and force of the production took many by surprise on the tour of Britain. Lesley Sharp recalls that to some audiences it must have seemed that a cast of eight were going crazy on stage:

'I think some people didn't quite know what to do with it. When you go to somewhere like Stratford-upon-Avon, the audiences are more easily led into your convention. In Harlow, they like an easier evening. We were all pretty vile. It wasn't easy on the eye, or easy on the ears. There were times in places like Milton Keynes when you felt that you were slogging your guts out'.

The language was often violent (Agrafena tells her daughter, Lipochka, that if she doesn't stop practising her dancing before breakfast, then 'I'll bash your head against that table just as if I was a peasant threshing wheat'). But it was the extremeness of the characterisations which, when delivering Dear's script under Donnellan's direction, culminated in extraordinary performances.

Timothy Walker played the part of the Uriah Heap-ish, vodka-alcoholic solicitor, with greasy hair and disgusting personal hygiene, 'all zits and nits' (Simon Trussler Plays & Players July 1988 Donmar Warehouse). His character was partially based in fact. On the first day of rehearsals, Walker arrived with a photograph of a group of nineteenth century Russian merchants. At the back of the group was a figure sporting the lank hair that Walker adopted for Rispolozhensky. Walker protests that he would never have animated that picture of a possible Rispolozhensky until he had discovered the character in rehearsal:

'A piece of direction that helped me enormously came from an idea which I didn't know what to do with. I somehow arrived at the possibility of Rispolozhensky having his own vodka glass. I don't know why I thought it, but I thought: "Maybe I've got it in my pocket". Once I'd had the idea I wrapped it in brown paper because he was an alcoholic. I might have said that to another director who would have dismissed the idea as ridiculous. But because it had come from something within me which had been released by my feelings, Declan was then able to take that idea and build on it. I remember taking out my big idea in one rehearsal – it was so embarrassing – unwrapping the paper and thinking I'd have to justify it further by saying he was a complete hypochondriac and thus wouldn't share glasses. But Declan, with an insight which helped me, said: "The reason is so that he can ingratiate himself because he's not going to cause anyone any trouble". The moment he'd said that I realised it was a good idea. From making something of that came the whole idea of being ingratiating. The performance was built on something as small as that, then applied, to become an action that completely related to somebody else. It was about that interaction. Something as simple as that might fuel you for ten days'.

A combination of actors' instinct, the swing of the language, and Donnellan's demands on his team,

created the outrageous world of the play. Lesley Sharp also understands how it was achieved:

'The base line with Declan is that he starts with truth, with real truth. He builds up and makes you daring because he shows you just how far you can go with that truth. You can end up with something that is extremely funny and it may be overpowering; but nonetheless it is extremely truthful because it is based in real psychological complexity. He allows you to go as far as you possibly can so that you're not doing television performances, nor are you necessarily being subtle or careful with the truth. You're being bold. He's wonderful at seeing what you're doing, being excited by that, and then taking you further. Then *you* get excited and go further too. It wasn't just a Russian comedy that nobody understood. With great power, Declan and Nick Dear brought it into 1988'.

This wasn't made explicit with any cheap anachronism in set, costumes, props, or textual references. The themes were so poignant for a 1988 audience that no relocation or new clothes were needed for the play to become a product of our own age. 'There aren't any anachronistic references in *A Family Affair* quite deliberately,' says Dear,

'but inevitably there's a tone to the writing which is something to do with the way I'm writing now. It's been said to me that translations and adaptations have a lifespan of about a decade or so. Then they start to look of their time. If we look at a translation done in the fifties, the word "frightful" pops up all the time. It's not to make a point. It's because that's the way people talked and should have talked. They look dated in the extreme now and no doubt mine will look old-fashioned in twenty years time. You do it for an immediate response, for now, for a performance, not really in the expectation that it will get more'.

In adapting, Nick Dear formed a second career (*A Family Affair* earned him an Olivier Award nomination too, for Outstanding Achievement, in memory of Kenneth Tynan) as his terrific *Last Days of Don Juan* for the RSC illustrates. *A Family Affair* itself has been produced abroad in Australia and in America (the Philadelphia production, directed by a Russian, was a huge hit) as well as a not so good production by Manchester Contact and a successful production at the Edinburgh Lyceum. Ostrovsky was known to the British stage prior to *A Family Affair* – most notably through his play *The Storm*. But it was *A Family Affair* that set a minor Ostrovsky revival into motion, notably Richard Jones' production of *Too Clever By Half* at the Old Vic in 1989, with Richard Hudson's distorted set and Alex Jennings' leering smart-ass influencing a number of productions of unrelated plays ever since.

By fortuitously using Nick Dear, Cheek by Jowl confirmed its reputation as a leading light of European classic revivals and renewals. Through an apparent haphazardness in their dramaturgy, they come across the right plays at the right time. For Cheek by Jowl it was important to maintain the momentum, and the media hype that had accompanied winning the Society of West End Theatre's 1987 Director of the Year Olivier Award for *The Cid*, *Twelfth Night* and *Macbeth*. With *A Family Affair*, they couldn't have wished for anything better, anything more politically timely, or anything so seriously, shrewdly funny.

This is vintage Cheek by Jowl in that it takes a neglected classic, strips it of antique formality and makes it plain that the ironic exploration of a moral dilemma is the binding factor in great drama down the ages (Michael Billington *Guardian* 5/12/88 Donmar Warehouse)

Philoctetes hadn't been seen in Britain since the 1960's when Colin Blakely played the role for Olivier's Old Vic. After Cheek by Jowl's production, the play received a new treatment in Seamus Heaney's *The Cure at Troy* for Ireland's Field Day, coming to Kilburn's Tricycle Theatre in London, 1991. It's a peculiarly powerful play.

It is about a man with a disease in his foot inflicted by displeased gods. He has been marooned on the island of Lemnos by the Greeks, who left him with a bow and arrows that they now want back to win the Trojan War. After the death of Achilles, Philoctetes' friend, a prophet, has foretold that the War can only be won with that magic bow.

Philoctetes, and those Greeks – Odysseus and Neoptolemus – all think themselves strong-willed. The play reveals them to be unable to cope with themselves, let alone have relationships with other people. Neoptolemus – Achilles' son, Odysseus' protégé, and the bright young hope of Greece's future – falls into a special kind of love with Philoctetes, wishing to devote the rest of his life to him to sweeten his bitterness.

It is a play of great human depth; but it also shows how a personal impulse can be an act of public subversion. Sophocles sends in a god, Heracles, to sort things out, and not upset the censors of his day – even though bringing in the *deus ex machina* would have only made the ironies even more apparent to the audience, drawing attention to them, not craftily solving them.

Philoctetes played in repertory with *The Tempest*. It wasn't just the sharing of an island setting which brought them together – though this simple fact

was used to calm the suspicious Eastern Bloc cultural ministries, who allowed the pair of plays to tour in the Spring of 1989. It was the parallel themes of social, political, and personal dispossession, and of the choices and hypocritical dogmas, which both plays' sets of characters explore.

Where *The Tempest* was a free-for-all of theatricality and instinctive impulses, *Philoctetes* was far calmer, far more rational, the discoveries of the story made by a linear rather than a tangential progression. Paddy Cunneen's music – his first commission for Cheek by Jowl after some years as Glen Walford's Associate at the Liverpool Everyman – echoed the contrast between the two productions. In the *Tempest*, it played whatever hectic tune the action and atmosphere prompted, from rap to music hall, traditional jazz to abstract improvisation, brash melodies to cacophonous harmonies. In *Philoctetes*, it was far darker, with complex three-part vocal music (the pungent, triadic harmonies of which took plenty of additional Saturday morning rehearsals to master) with the actor Lloyd Owen's richly resonant, deep bass voice grounding the group of sailors into a strong ensemble.

Cunneen's music in Cheek by Jowl's recent productions has often had a bonding effect upon the performers. Just as Jane Gibson's movement was to become an essential but indistinguishable ingredient of the whole, Cunneen's musical skills (while obviously a welcome additional talent) were in keeping with the whole Cheek by Jowl approach. Duncan Duff (a sailor and then the god Heracles in *Philoctetes*) describes Cunneen's swift acceptance by and of the company:

'Paddy was invaluable. He added another dimension. He became part of the Cheek by Jowl furniture. There's now no differentiation between a music and a dramatic rehearsal; they're closely integrated. Paddy was neither precious nor fazed by being at the heart of things'.

That company spirit which Cheek by Jowl intangibly engenders – never forced, never twee, never a false smile – was something Michael Coveney must have noticed in Prague. He could be forgiven if he'd felt slightly timid of the company with whom he shared the same Czechoslovakian hotel courtesy of the British Council, since he'd just been especially

critical of *Philoctetes* at the Donmar Warehouse in the arts' pages of the *Financial Times*. But the company (of whom Timothy Walker was the most assiduous of review-readers) were not in the least bit hostile or cool towards Coveney. They welcomed him with open arms. Both parties appreciate that reviews and criticism are rarely personal slights, usually considered responses to professional creativity.

In Prague, as then in Bucharest, *The Tempest* was a riotous political allegory for the country's suffering under sedentary Stalinism (Vaclav Havel had been arrested once again). Duncan Duff appreciates that the more sober *Philoctetes* presented profound problems of conscience for the audience to mull over. Where *The Tempest* demanded an immediate response, *Philoctetes*, perhaps, provoked a long-term consideration well after the event. Duff recognised this:

> 'The idea of obeying your duty to the state was very much understood, as was the notion of following your personal conscience – Neoptolemus wrestles with that dichotomy. The audiences in Eastern Europe were the best I've played to, as the plays meant something that we can't appreciate in England'.

A political provocateur abroad, *Philoctetes* in Britain was more of a morality play. Some recognised that this was because of Kenneth McLeish's translation. A respected writer and translator hitherto (and afterwards commissioned by Deborah Warner for the RSC's *Electra*, by Donnellan and Ormerod for their *Peer Gynt* at the National, by Katie Mitchell for *Women of Troy* at the Gate, Notting Hill and, with Frederick Raphael, by Manchester's Royal Exchange for *Medea*) McLeish penned a translation which was, according to the *Daily Telegraph*'s Charles Spencer:

> 'Both colloquial and dignified [. . .] The audience is left to draw contemporary parallels without tiresome directorial nudging' (5/12/88 Donmar Warehouse)

(a passing swipe at *The Tempest*'s 'particularly dismal example of directors' theatre' in Spencer's view (*Daily Telegraph* 28/11/88).)

Philoctetes in Britain, and particularly in London, was liked by those who hated, and hated by those

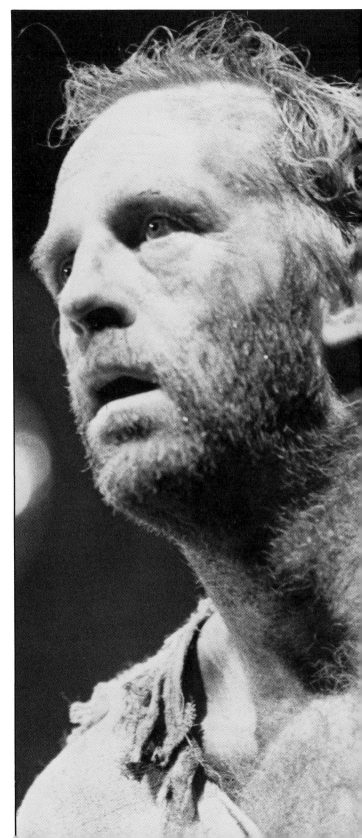

who loved, *The Tempest*. British audience taste seems more singular than the diverse palate of audiences abroad. But perhaps Cheek by Jowl was asking for trouble by playing these two plays side by side. Those who gave a lukewarm response to *Philoctetes* were perhaps nonplussed by its relative cool-headedness alongside the hot-blooded tempestuousness of the other production. Perhaps they felt the whole was diluted by some of its parts.

As Charlie Roe's officer Odysseus (soon to be exposed as far from a gentleman) intoned 'This is the coast of Lemnos', the company screeched like gulls, and a sailor walked briskly around the perimeter of the stage letting his handfuls of sand fall through his fingers. A nice idea (its abstract theatreness, and the physical line of divide that it left, acted as a framing device) yet some thought it a hackneyed Cheek by Jowl gag. Those sailors were, to many, too gaily attired in their *South Pacific*-like, pristine-white bell-bottoms and blue-trimmed smocks. Thinking it more 'Hello Sailor' than Ancient Greece, some people were irritated. For others:

> 'Cheek by Jowl as a company scratch beneath the mould of an antique to find live dramatic roots' (Oliver Taplin *Times Literary Supplement* 16/12/88 Donmar Warehouse).

There was the simpleness of Ormerod's design – oil drums, oars and blankets for Philoctetes' cave; a shield hanging from the ceiling at the back of the stage, descending to be taken by a naked Duncan Duff with a helmet and sword as Heracles – which added a quality to the atmosphere in which the performers had room to breathe:

> 'This is its first venture into Greek tragedy, but it brings to it exactly the same assumptions that it brought to the world of French classicism; namely the belief that flesh-and-blood characters lurk under the heroic gestures, and that style is not a starting point but a reward for getting the characters right' (Irving Wardle *Times* 5/12/88 Donmar Warehouse).

The spotless white uniforms of the Greek sailors contrasted with the rags of the rugged Philoctetes (Keith Bartlett) and his apparent abuse of the bow the Greeks seek by using it as a crutch. Donnellan expanded upon the internal contrasts of the plays in interview:

> 'Both plays are about men who've been deserted on islands because they've been thought unfit for society. Philoctetes has been quarantined on the island because he has a disease which irrationally terrifies all the Greeks – it's to do with magic, not with reason.

> 'Like Prospero, Philoctetes and Neoptolemus fight their way throughout the play to start again. They learn to love in the space of the play. They learn to forgive. Neoptolemus has to defy everything he's been brought up to believe. He's placed in this extraordinarily modern position in which he has to choose between what the government tells him to be right and what he believes to be right. He devotes his life to Philoctetes, a diseased, old, bitter, unattractive and not at all morally superior man, someone who's full of self-pity and someone who is in every respect fantastically ugly – inside, outside, upside-down. Neoptolemus has to go to the State, embodied by Odysseus in his clean underpants, and say: "No, your way is not for me". It's a wild and outrageous act of subversion' (*Plays International* November 1988).

Pride, honour, political expediency – the individual versus the smooth but corrupt society. Paterson Joseph as Neoptolemus gave a dignified yet heart-rending performance.

Again a *Guardian* reviewer outside London made a call for an award for the production (*Philoctetes* had already won first prize in the LWT Plays on Stage Award, a substantial sum of £15,000 making the production possible):

> '*Philoctetes* won first prize at the Dionysiad of 409 BC. If this production doesn't win some of the prizes going in 1988–9 AD, then Olympus is barren and the gods unjust' (M. Grosvenor-Meyer *Guardian* 17/10/88 Theatre Royal Bury St Edmunds).

Yet the *Oracle* teletext at the time was transmitting Patrick Marmion's sage words: 'The production fails to confront the play's antique machismo leaving it a thinking man's *Rambo*, dressed as a theatrical experiment'.

With Cheek by Jowl's next production, *The Doctor of Honour*, macho gore took centre stage with a vengeance.

money that they now receive to fledgling companies just as Cheek by Jowl were in 1981). They are its *raison d'être* and it is theirs. Thus all the productions have been directed and designed by Donnellan and Ormerod. Except one. Lindsay Posner, with the designer Julian McGowan, were the first, and – though their production was a success and well-liked by Donnellan and Ormerod – are the last director and designer other than the co-Artistic Directors to create a Cheek by Jowl production.

The Posner/McGowan 1989 production was, in a sense, a breather for Donnellan and Ormerod. Cheek by Jowl had certain obligations to fulfil in terms of its Arts Council touring schedule, which Donnellan and Ormerod themselves could not meet since they were rehearsing their debut production for the National Theatre. One would imagine that the pressure of potentially detrimental and inevitable comparison with their employers must have been a great strain for the employees. But the guest artistic team took it in their stride, allowing others to worry about judging dissimilarities while they just got on with the job of rehearsing and producing a Spanish Golden Age classic. Their mentors were doing the same with a parallel play, Lope de Vega's *Fuente Ovejuna*, at the National's Cottesloe Theatre.

Inviting Lindsay Posner to direct was no blind date for Cheek by Jowl. Posner, momentarily a disillusioned RADA-trained actor after graduating in English from Exeter University, had joined Cheek by Jowl as Donnellan's Assistant Director in 1985, once the tour of *A Midsummer Night's Dream* was already underway. Posner has strong views of his own – apparently he and Donnellan would end up rehearsing in separate rooms because he refused to keep quiet – yet it was probably the strength of this artistic vision, coupled with his contrasting, dry temperament, that attracted Donnellan to him in the first place. He assisted on *The Man of Mode* and later on Donnellan and Ormerod's production of *Romeo and Juliet* at Regent's Park's Open Air Theatre in 1986.

Posner then joined the Royal Court as an Associate Director under Max Stafford-Clark, directing a very different repertoire of new British plays at the

hile imitation may be a sincere form of flattery, nobody can do it quite like DD – so they don't try. They take on board their predecessor's most valuable lesson – less can mean more – but stamp their own authority upon this seventeenth century Spanish Renaissance Drama (Lyn Gardner *City Limits* 4/5/89 Donmar Warehouse)

Cheek by Jowl is no more and no less than the product of the creativity of Declan Donnellan and Nick Ormerod. Their administrator, Barbara Matthews, is the first to admit that were those two to depart, Cheek by Jowl would cease to exist in all but name (and they all hope that were such a situation to arise, the Arts Council would reallocate the

Court's struggling Theatre Upstairs (it was temporarily closed for virtually a year, 1989–1990, because of lack of funding). It was thus in ironic circumstances that he was invited to direct for Cheek by Jowl.

Posner, like many directors of his young generation, would not treat a new work any differently from a classic: the text is paramount; the most important people in the production are those on stage, the actors. So, Posner felt that there was no contradiction in being associated with the Court and yet going off to direct a European Classic for his parent company, just at the moment that his new guardian was in trouble. One of the maxims at the Court has always been to direct new plays like classics and classics like new plays. 'My ideal,' argues Posner,

> 'is a challenging play that is a physical as well as an intellectual experience. It's quite hard to find the right combination because there has tended to be a polarisation: lots of new work has been dull on the physical side of things and has been very text-based in its presentation; whereas "designer classics" have moved into an area which has come off the text a bit and has been very physically-based, sometimes at the expense of intellectual and exploratory depth. In that sense, both are negative and there needs to be a balance'.

Posner thus approached Calderon's wife-murder tragedy – the type of extreme story we might read about in the tabloid press: chilling, terrifying, yet gripping, even titillating; with subversive political undercurrents of a hypocritical code of honour – with the same aplomb as he would a new work.

Posner shares with Donnellan a concern with the telling of a story through the medium of the performer alone (*The Doctor of Honour*'s sole prop was a candle), an instinctive physicality, mixing deft craft with simple art. With a play like *The Doctor of Honour* (the title modified from poet Roy Campbell's original title to his elegant yet raw translation, *The Surgeon of His Honour*) the dark emotions, combined with the bleak environment, could result in an entirely barren dramatic experience. The play is certainly uncompromising. Indeed, in initial discussions about which of Posner's short-list of fifteen

Spanish Golden Age plays he should direct (*The Surgeon of His Honour* had been produced once before in a student production by the pioneering Drama Centre in London's Chalk Farm), Posner recalls the concern about the impact of the brutal ending, wondering what exactly was being condemned in the cynical redemption of the wife-murderer Don Gutierre, who is obliged by a morally suspect King to marry his wronged former mistress, Dona Leonor (who asks how she feels?) as recompense for murdering his wife, Dona Mencia.

The world of the play is a patriarchy. Women are helpless, in the hands of a fate dictated to them by men:

> 'In Seville I was born, and there
> Henry first saw me, thawed my cold disdain
> With loving praise – O happy Star! – and then
> He went on duty. When my father
> Cut short the liberty I once enjoyed,
> To put me in a convent, as I feared, –
> I gave my hand to Don Gutierre. Then
> Henry returned. I love him: yet my honour
> Forbids. That's all I know about myself' (Dona Mencia).

The masculine, imposed codes of honour and retribution (or revenge) thus come under scrutiny, Calderon questioning the behaviour that produces madness and innocent death. The uncomfortable resolution of the play is not a dashed off ending by a dramatist keen to finish his umpteenth stage play, suggests Posner, but a hugely questionable smothering of guilt, smoothing it over, by a shaky and thus paranoiacally manipulative political system (embodied by an imperfect king), scared that private dishonour will receive a foul public reception. The two, private and public, are, in practice, inextricably linked. Dona Leonor at the end of Act I simply states:

> 'Since I have lost my name
> There's nothing for me but to die'.

There's no distinction between the personal and the public since in any bourgeois, self-promoting power-group, they amount to the same thing. Calderon's play is thus not about the peculiar obsessions of an historically past Spanish aristocracy, but dealing with the concerns of any ruling class at any time, where the potential damage to one's reputation needs to be kept secret. Calderon uses an extreme example of wrong-doing to highlight the everyday derring-do of a corroding political system.

That system was visually manifested in the staging. It was intense and formal, some might say ascetic, purposefully utilising Cheek by Jowl's hallmark of chairs lined up at the back of the stage in which the actors sat bolt upright when not performing. There was a rigidity in the choreographed movement too (movement consultant: Geraldine Stephenson) as the company's emotional manoeuvres across the black and white chessboard floor created a paradox of passion versus total restraint, rarely touching physically as they spoke to each other across the expanse of the bare stage, revolving around a single, central column – a 'phallus' in Lyn Gardner's vivid interpretation for *City Limits* (4/5/89 Donmar Warehouse); 'a lone stumpy tiled obelisk to signify a wall, a castle, and a place to plant the bloody hand of death', according to Michael Coveney in *The Financial Times* (28/4/89 Donmar Warehouse); or used to 'hide eavesdroppers, aspiring adulterers and self-righteous snoops' as *The Independent*'s Georgina Brown observed (27/4/89, Donmar Warehouse).

'The small company had to create a world with a minimum of props and a minimum of set requirements,' explains Posner:

'That is a Cheek by Jowl aesthetic which I inherited, which is always partly to do with economics and partly to do with aesthetic theory. Obviously a touring company can't lug big structures around with them. On the other hand, both Declan and myself are quite minimal with shows: maximum actor ability and minimum prop and set structure'.

Like Donnellan, with composer Paddy Cunneen, in the quintessentially Spanish *Fuente Ovejuna* at the National (and as Cheek by Jowl had done to some extent in *The Cid*), Posner used guitar music to enhance the Spanish atmosphere. Unlike Donnellan and Cunneen – whose live guitar music at the National seemed to come organically from the production, as the manifestation of the spirit of the rallying community – Posner's interludes were taped, keeping the performers distanced within a rarefied Spanish ambience. Yet the harsh world was discoloured by the lush richness of the costumes – black, crimson and golden crushed velvet, significantly bruised in effect, 'like a painting by Velázquez come to life' (Catherine Cain *Watford Observer* 17/3/89 Old Town Hall Hemel Hempstead – Velázquez was, of course, a contemporary of Calderon, a Court painter in the 1620's and 1630's. Calderon wrote *El Medico de su Honra* in 1635). The costumes did not give the impression of a lavish, ripe decadence, but of an ever-present, malignant horror. This reflects the coolness of Calderon's calculating text.

Calderon's speeches demand a stand-and-deliver bravery on the part of the actor when thrusting forth their arguments. Resisting the temptation by many actors to emote profusely at the expense of meaning, Posner drilled his actors to be dispassionate and unemotional, playing the argument of the play from which the passion would then emerge willy-nilly. Emotion would exist in a vacuum if the thought didn't come first. Rick Fisher's lighting design ('a delicate essay in chiaroscuro' enthused Michael Coveney in *The Financial Times* (28/4/89)) highlighted and focused the arguments of the play's characters even more by compelling the audience to concentrate upon the actor, as a single spotlight would be drawn in upon a soliloquising face, words offset only by a dramatic ruff.

Posner makes no excuses for his rigorous ensemble work. Even were the play not about a rigid social system, regimented by strict codes, he would employ such a technique:

'Obviously it's the actors who contribute and it's the actor who performs. But if the actors are directed very specifically, and the director has a strong vision – a vision which can embrace the particular contributions from the actors – then that actually releases the actors into something that's ultimately very liberating. If actors are directed specifically and in a detailed way, then they grow on top of something that's very strong and rooted for them, giving them great security in performance. You've got to be sensitive to when someone can contribute positively and imaginatively, and to be able to use that and to mould it. In the end, a strong vision from a director is very exciting. You can always see that in a production'.

Generally, Posner's production was well-received, despite Richard Edwards' reservations in *The Birmingham Post*:

'There is not much action – which is unforgivable for a company that can turn a play into a whirlwind of business' (23/3/89 Midlands Arts Centre, Canon Hill Park).

Jane Edwardes writing in *Time Out* made a more usual, favourable comparison:

'Surprisingly, director Lindsay Posner, stepping into Donnellan's shoes, has been able to adopt the C by J house style seemingly effortlessly without constraining his own dramatic invention' (3/5/89 Donmar Warehouse).

Posner himself feels that his production was his own. It could never have been a Cheek by Jowl production *de facto*, since it was not Declan Donnellan and Nick Ormerod's:

'Every show is infused to an extent with the personality of the director. The director is a strong force. People say "you're realising the play" when the production's successful, which is nonsense. Plays don't have their own voice. It's a mixture between the directing, the acting and the writing which produces a particular flavour in a production. There was a difference in tone with other Cheek by Jowl productions. I always perceive Declan's spirit as something very celebratory, particularly when he does comedies. Whereas, I suppose, this was quite savage and hard for a Cheek by Jowl production'.

While savagery and harshness are not alien to a Donnellan/Ormerod production, they are never exclusive qualities. With *Sara*, for example, Cheek by Jowl demonstrated how they could be employed for cruel fun, and to wicked effect.

ideals to plunge the depths of the *sturm und drang* of domestic drama. It had a contemporary scenario, not taken from the mythological past to give an historical perspective on the present, and was written in present-day prose rather than lofty verse. While Cheek by Jowl had shown that there is more than meets the eye in the French classical plays, they were equally to acknowledge the historical and cultural significance of the retitled *Sara* through the style of production, presenting two worlds in stark contrast.

Why the play so suited their own brand of English irony, which had both thrilled and perplexed the critics of their eighties' work, was because Lessing had chosen eighteenth century middle-class England as the setting of his play: a boarding house in Dover as the centre of the action, with the characters' names plucked from the novels of Richardson and the comic plays of Congreve. It was England observed with an ironical detachment from abroad.

Here were the pre-echoes of melodrama: a bourgeois tragi-comedy, the audience's imaginations more likely to be stirred by that which is instantly recognisable as repugnant while inviting sympathy. The suicidal impulses which the extremes of passion within the play depict come from a society on the edge of its reason. Cheek by Jowl explored that society as much as the characters. (Irving Wardle in the *Independent on Sunday* called it: 'A Restoration comedy turned inside out' (10/6/90 Lilian Baylis).)

Paddy Cunneen's underscore (his compositions are never negatively referred to as incidental music) became a part of the way the actors moved on the stage. It enhanced their posture, as Jane Gibson appreciated:

'I did a lot of eighteenth century dance with Paddy's baroque music, which is superb to move to. We worked through the dance – not that they danced in performance; but being able to dance like that, which is quite a demanding technique because it's beginning to go towards ballet, is the complete opposite of how our bodies are now. So rather than say: "Stand up, get your chest out, drop your shoulders", we listened to baroque music with its wonderful sweeping curves. We moved through the curves and opened the body

Space is created by a moving constellation of actors on the barren boards, the only fixed point being a singular armchair, rather than the finite lines of boxed scenery. Scenes straddle each other as if still interleaved like the pages of a book, superimposing themselves upon the imagination – an accumulative process (Steven Wasserman *Cambridge Weekly Review* 2/5/90 Cambridge Arts Theatre)

It is often claimed that what is English about English Drama is the tragedy that lurks beneath the comic mask. You see it in Restoration comedy; you see it in Ayckbourn. How did Cheek by Jowl see it in an eighteenth century German play?

G. E. Lessing, the founder of modern dramaturgy, wrote *Miss Sara Sampson* in 1755. It was a turning point in dramatic history, rejecting the very stoicism of a French dramatic tradition that Cheek by Jowl had explored in *Andromache* and *The Cid*, breaking the shackles of an expectation of a decorum of high

out and allowed the body to present itself, though not in an arrogant way. You give the actors the experience so then they see the relationship between the text and that way of moving. The text is full of curves and curls in its big phrases, like a piece of baroque movement or music'.

Cunneen relished the fact that the play came at a time in history when music was shifting from the baroque to the classical:

'The inherent characteristic of the musical period was *sturm und drang*, the thing which allegedly Haydn started off, the use of minor keys and that more pent up style of playing. That *sturm und drang* movement is what Lessing started in literature. I suppose it is melodramatic now, but it was very shocking in its day. We're all used to this sense of baroque proportionality or classically balanced construction now; those emotional chords screaming their way in was very shocking at the time.

'Some of the choices you make are as a result of an intellectual analysis of the material you're working with. But because the function of the music is to be emotional, I don't think that you can achieve it by purely analytical means. There's a lot of: "Oh this'll be good here. I can't tell you why", and you try it.

'I wanted to do things like Haydn or Mozart string quartets because they are really gritty. The Cheek by Jowl compromise was a 'cello and a violin – I wanted them to use enough rosin to really bite into their strings – but that was great because Duncan Duff could play the clarinet so we tucked him in there as well. For the father, Daniel Thorndike's Sir William Sampson, the music was much like a Bach two-part invention. When we played the music it just seemed to lift the whole thing in terms of mood and period feel. What started out as Declan saying: "I don't think there'll be a great deal of music in this" and me saying "I agree", ended up as nailing music across all the scenes and supporting it here, there, and everywhere'.

The whole production was centred around one chair on Ormerod's bare-boards set, the characters sweeping around it, and the whole perimeter of the stage, overlapping each others' entrances and exits

(for which Paddy Cunneen's string duo would surge menacingly) in concentric figures of eight,

'that marked the relentless pursuit of Sara, the circling of an eagle above its prey' (Alfredo Goldstein *El Dia* 23/4/90 Millington Drake Theatre Montevideo) –

a bold visual image. The large leatherbound chair and a small plain table, with only a slanting beam at a 45° angle to suggest claustrophobic interiors, contrasted with the rich, fashionable clothes of the characters, who would showily pick up their petticoats, flick their tailcoats, and be fussily spruced up for each scene by their servants (with far more genuine dedication than in *Andromache*). The frozen attitudes of their assumed poses would break into the steamy passion of the play:

'The fashion-plate tableau dissolves, leaving Raad Rawi's Mellefont alone on stage with a sleeping servant whom he brutally kicks awake. The style at once defines a moment of historical change, and the conversion of decorative movement into a martial art' (Irving Wardle *Independent on Sunday* 10/6/90 Lilian Baylis).

Jane Gibson's movement released the performers physically, freeing their emotional expression. The attitudes were adopted by the characters in order to then break free from them, to fight to destroy others through their words, ultimately a self-destructive pursuit. Their words attempted to change the thoughts of the other characters, as Cheek by Jowl attempt to project the words directly to the audience, speaking to them not for them.

Using a turn-of-the-century translation by Ernest Bell, with adept modification by Donnellan and for which this 'newcomer' Bell received much praise for his colloquialisms (his is a name which one suspects is too good to be true, since the script's both earnest and clear as a bell), the *Sara* cast were able to play upon the contrast between the world of the formal past and the world of the desperate present and future. The translation subverted eighteenth century and its own late Victorian tastes, but it was dated enough for us to appreciate the age of the play as alien to our own, though appreciate the modernity of its themes:

'Through this complex drama we arrive at a living image of another age. We recognise, as in a dis-

torted mirror, our own selves with distinct new features' (Jorge Arias *La Republica* 27/4/90 Millington Drake Theatre Montevideo).

The core of the subversion was in the sexual hypocrisy – the manipulative Marwood (a brilliant piece of passion from Sheila Gish) determined to thwart her estranged lover's lust for the naive girl Sara, whose father was equally determined to disown this girl, who, in ways less blasé than Marwood's unmarried motherhood, ignored the conventional duties of her own time. Inevitably there were many comparisons with *Les Liaisons Dangereuses*, and more particularly, and in Uruguay especially, to *Dangerous Liaisons* the American film version of Christopher Hampton's staging of Laclos' novel. *Sara* was a baroque ('beauty compressed but almost breaking the bounds of control', as the programme notes quoted) *Fatal Attraction*:

'Furtively sinister with flashes of humour and eroticism' (Michael Coveney *Observer* 10/6/90 Lilian Baylis).

In Uruguay, the production was likened to that country's popular sport:

'Each moment was an episode in a cock-fight' (Alfredo Goldstein *El Dia* 23/4/90 Millington Drake Theatre).

When performing at the Connaught Theatre, Worthing, Sheila Gish's knicker elastic snapped half-way through a scene. She elegantly whipped them up into her hands as she found them lying round her ankles. In a sense, it was prophetic, since the sexual, seedy tensions (without wishing to denigrate Gish's underwear) inevitably reach breaking point as all are self-destructive.

The play frequently has long, soul-searching, self-pitying and breast-thumping, brow-beating speeches, manipulating the affections of the listener by going to such lengths to describe themselves (a favourite pursuit of Cheek by Jowl is to find what compels a character to keep talking, and others to listen without interrupting). It's powerful stuff, and Cheek by Jowl's production didn't let up in its psychological torture, the heat boiling beneath the cool exterior. They are rich, confident sentences, but sometimes expressing an emotion larger than the speaker can cope with:

'Movement, whether stiff or explosive, is crucial to the production, not simply because it checks the torrent of words but also because it lets real feelings out from under the verbal burden. Here the two women are vital: Rachel Joyce's Sara, tense to the finger-tips, rushing and drawing back in her thinly veiled insecurity; Sheila Gish's Marwood, stage-managing some of her own outbursts and yet at the very edge of breakdown. When the two women finally meet, what could easily be a wordy quarrel becomes a collision between two sets of jangling nerves, two brands of vulnerability' (Philip Brady *Times Literary Supplement* 15/6/90 Lilian Baylis).

Donnellan is particularly tuned into directing women. Rachel Joyce, who had played Laurencia in *Fuente Ovejuna* at the National the previous year, and who played Sara, sees this as one of Donnellan's many fortes:

'He's unafraid of, and very interested in, the relationships between women. They're so special – there's nothing like them. On stage, too often you get drawn into playing one aspect of life, which tends to be the love story between the man and the woman. Declan appreciates that life is more complex than that'.

Joyce remembers both the movement and the music being crucial to facilitating the production, the midwife to the play:

'Right at the beginning of rehearsals we put on the huge skirts and were experimenting with those huge figure-of-eight patterns, following one another in the restrained dignity of that movement. All the time we were trying to find the lid that was put on top of all that passion and the way the characters could do that.

'There's never anything decorative in Declan's productions; things are always there to move the piece on. Paddy's music was partly there as a break from all that dialogue and the intensity of that emotion – often by working against it. At moments of potential over-the-top melodrama, the music would also be highly emotional, thus relieving the text from the danger of becoming wishy-washy. By admitting the tear-jerks of the text through the music, the sniggering behind the hands in the audience was avoided'.

The imaginative association of the play with the contrasting visual as well as aural images, was due in part – as with *The Doctor of Honour* – to Rick Fisher's meticulous lighting design. Footlights thrust the company into silhouette, both sombre and sinister as is the play. In Montevideo, where *Sara* was first performed, there were two power-cuts on the opening night – and not because Barbara Matthews was trying her hand at cueing the show though she'd be forgiven for momentarily thinking it was her who had fused the theatre and consequently the rest of Uruguay. The hosts provided four calor gas lanterns which were placed along the apron of the stage, in their own way acting as eighteenth century footlights. Despite the curious thrill for the performers of this atmosphere – enhanced perhaps by the fact that virtually the entire cast were suffering from a bout of salmonella – it must have been frustrating for Fisher because it lost the diversity and contrasts of his original design, such as:

'Side-lights pinpointing faces with a desperate gleam. When Sara dies, her white shift is picked out from the darkness while her cries are offset by a servant mumbling the 23rd Psalm. It's simple and astonishing: very Cheek by Jowl' (Gwyn Morgan *Plays & Players* August 1990 Lilian Baylis).

All the despairing deaths at the end of the play were, for some, a little implausible, overblown in their tragedy, destroying the fine balance between tragedy and comedy that had gone before. Cheek by Jowl's next production was *Hamlet*, a tragedy chock-full of comedy and with a ridiculous bloodbath of all and sundry towards the end. Like *Sara*, Cheek by Jowl's three Shakespearian tragedies confront the problems of tone with shocking simplicity.

RESTLESS
ECSTASY

TRAGEDY

Simply staged and spoken at conversational level, this little production by the touring Cheek by Jowl company may lose the grandeur and most of the poetry, but its direct focus on those individual tragedies makes it one of the most harrowing *Othello*s I have ever seen (Anthony Masters *Times* 24/3/83 New End Theatre, Hampstead)

Othello, Cheek by Jowl's second production in 1982, was the first Shakespeare that they presented. Shakespeare productions don't make up the majority of Cheek by Jowl's work, but they do make up the major part (eight out of eighteen, including *As You Like It*). Shakespeare, Sophocles, Thackeray or Lessing – they've all been coherently simple in design, simple in delivery.

Those who have delighted in the irreverance of *Twelfth Night* and *A Midsummer Night's Dream*, or the outrageousness of the freely roaming *Tempest* ('the thought is free') may query the simplicity tag. It's clear that with tragedies like *Macbeth* and *Hamlet* there has been less apparent frivolity and creative clutter. On the other hand, '*Othello* was very proppy,' recalls Donnellan,

'with teacups and glasses and furniture. It was done in hard modern dress. It had a very oppressive, domestic atmosphere'.

Ormerod adds:

'*Othello* does seem to work well in a claustrophobic, domestic, specific world'.

As for the telling of a Shakespeare story – tragedy, comedy or romance – all of Cheek by Jowl's sophistication is rooted in the simple craft of the actor. It is the same actor's imagination running wild and causing riotous action on stage that creates the seriousness of tragic demeanour.

Othello is a prime example where the two types of approach meet: the stillness and concentration of a soul-searching soliloquy; the zest of knock-about humour when Cassio gets drunk. Contrasting styles within a production is the result of the play's text. To clarify the meaning you simply have to follow through the thought of the words.

Anthony Masters, like many after him, was impressed with the pared down staging but disappointed that, to his ears, it made the poetry too urbane or ironic. With a Cheek by Jowl Shakespeare, your ears become attuned to a clarity of meaning. Character and story supersede a purple aesthetic of good verse-speaking. It's not necessarily the poetry that is lost, but a poetical notion of glamorous histrionics to which, sadly, our ears have become accustomed. If it sounds ironic in its innuendo compared with the tunes of old, then that's as much a reflection upon those ageing songs as it is on the new music. Harmonies in verse are as important as melodies.

Cheek by Jowl never strives to present the familiar, knowing what familiarity can breed. Yet the clarity of diction of their work makes it accessible to all – story and characters make sense because their words are their own, not a recollec-

tion of a flamboyant set speech from a drama school audition, or an 'O' level prac. crit.

Amanda Harris, who joined Cheek by Jowl straight from the Arts Educational Drama School in June 1982 to play Desdemona (mischievously doubling as the whore, Bianca), enthuses about her first professional engagement (which is not a dewy-eyed nostalgia, since she, like some other Cheek by Jowl performers, kept a notebook of the rehearsal gems and her excited feelings at the time). Certain things that Donnellan would give them as touchstones in rehearsal may seem common sense now. At the time, there were few directors who would approach plays in such a way, let alone be able to communicate it to a performer:

'Declan would say: "If you have an image in the words, you should actually see that image outside of yourself; you can picture it, and it's almost tangible". He gave it a name: External Stimulus. Your character can talk about it because she can see it. For instance, in *Othello*, "the green-eyed monster, jealousy" would be seen. Then it's frightening and you can react to it. You strip away all the fancy things behind an impulse to emote, to make it very simple; to just tell the story. It also gives the audience something to share, because you are taking it out to them. It gives the actor more colour and so you have a many-layered performance'.

It is the openness rather than introspection of performing which startled many at a Cheek by Jowl

production in the early eighties, something which we may have become used to now because the style has permeated the larger companies (not least because Donnellan and Ormerod themselves are working in mainstream theatre at the National). For theatre to constantly recreate itself, rather than merely reproduce, it must be fed by the innovation of the experimenting practitioners. 'Jowlies', as they affectionately call themselves with knowing self-mockery, are dotted around British theatre, bringing with them the experience, techniques and showmanship gained from a Cheek by Jowl production.

Nick Ormerod is not a showman. His modest designing influence upon a production is integral because it is a reflection of it; and this made itself apparent in the staging of *Othello*. On either side of an open stage stood a row of folding chairs which the performers would occupy when not in character. It wasn't some easy ensemble acting trick, giving the appearance of sustained involvement from the seven performers, but a deliberate focus for the audience, who shared the generously absorbed attentiveness of the actors. It is a sight to which Donnellan and Ormerod have returned in subsequent productions, and seems partially to arise, like so much of their work, from something experienced in rehearsal.

In any Cheek by Jowl rehearsal, even a re-rehearsal of a play some months into its run to refresh the company's creative impulses, it's always the case that 100% commitment, and total involvement, is required – not at the request of the director alone, but from the company as a whole. Amanda Harris enjoyed not having time to kill in any rehearsal: 'If you weren't there doing your bit, you'd be upstage making a noise or something'. Cheek by Jowl has never had spear-carriers to pad out a crowd scene. That use of actors as human scenery is redefined as a positive, contributory virtue in their productions.

Donnellan frequently claimed in interviews throughout the 1980's that he would enter a rehearsal room for each production without a clue what to do (as his experience grew, he knew what *not* to do). Far from being the confession of a weak director, devoid of ideas, it is the statement of one who will rarely prescribe, preferring to react to the spontaneous mood of the actors, who collectively create the atmosphere in the rehearsal room at any particular time. Thus, in *Othello* there could be harrowing tragedy in juxtaposition with significant humour, motivated by the actors' impetus. Roderigo entered in white shorts, a Hawaiian shirt and sunglasses, very much the loud English tourist, bulldozing his way around the *Costa del Sol*. There was the slapstick of the drinking scene, which turned into a party, with tipsy soldiers falling about in their Donald Duck and Mickey Mouse masks and army fatigues. This inventiveness spills over into more serious moments too, when extra business edifies the text. Desdemona was strangled by Othello with her own silk stocking – a seedy, jealous sex crime – while Emilia waited outside the bedroom, casually lighting a cigarette, the pain and futility of the tragic situation thus highlighted for the audience. And this image of Emilia recalled an earlier moment where Othello's 'flaming minister', as a concrete External Stimulus, had been his cigarette lighter.

The production toured for such an extensive time in two separate Autumn 1982 and Spring 1983 tours, and to over 40 venues around Britain, that many of the parts were re-cast. The part of Othello was played by two actors: first by the American, Doyle Richmond, and then by Ruddy L. Davis. What they had in common was that they were both black, which in itself is not that extraordinary now (though Michael Gambon, a white actor, arabbed himself up for Ayckbourn's 1990 Scarborough production).

Casting a black actor as Othello is not the most ambitious piece of integrated casting, though it was unusual enough to draw comment at the time. When Cheek by Jowl visited the public school bastion of the conservative establishment, Winchester, *The Wychemist News* reporter reflected an attitude woefully ingrained in Great Britain:

'It was easy for a Negro to sustain the thick-lipped accent consistently through the part, but the results were sometimes clumsy:

"An honest man he is and hates the slime,
That sticks on filtha deeds" ' (19/5/83).

Othello's casting isn't what the production will be remembered for primarily. It was a production that established Cheek by Jowl as an important and influential radical voice when it came to staging Shakespeare plays (in 1988 that phrase 'post-Cheek by Jowl manner' entered British theatre's vocabulary (David Edgar, *Independent* 2/1/88)).

As a cultural milestone, *Othello* was important. But only because the production was a good production. It's this, rather than its position in cultural history, which would satisfy Cheek by Jowl the most. Once again, Allen Saddler called provocatively from Plymouth Theatre Royal's Drum:

'For sheer pace, verve and, above all, clarity this production deserves an award' (*Guardian* 25/10/82).

With their next production, *Vanity Fair*, those calls began to be heeded.

A major factor in a Cheek by Jowl production, and this is especially true of their tragedies, is the way that the environment of the play's story, and the type of environment it depicts, is so sharply drawn that individuals' actions are given a distinct context. No Cheek by Jowl production is a vehicle for a starring lead. No play is left unexplored, no assumptions made. So *Othello* is not just about Othello, nor *Macbeth* Macbeth, nor *Hamlet* Hamlet. The productions reveal the circumstances that engender their personal tragedies. The tragedy belongs to humanity, not only to one man's vaulting ambition.

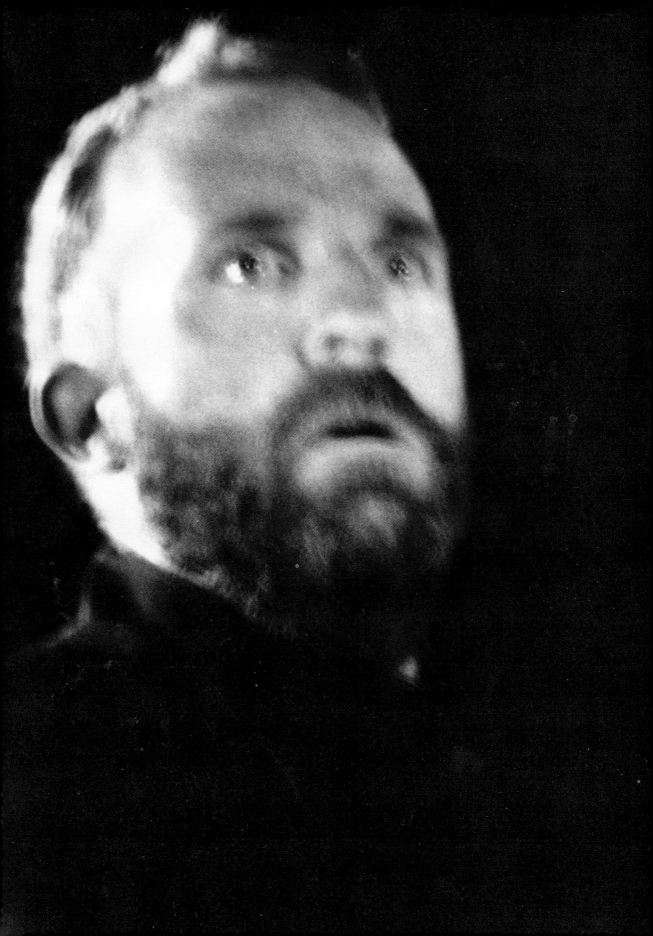

onnellan and his cast have restudied every dot and comma of one of the most familiar and hackneyed scripts in drama and have drawn from it a diamond-fresh interpretation of the play (Tom Vaughan *Morning Star* 23/11/87 Donmar Warehouse)

'Fuck off!' said Mrs Porter, and you couldn't dampen the brouhaha with soda water. The chatter was 'Porter, Porter' everywhere, and some didn't stop to think: 'IT'S SHOCKSPEARE' claimed the sober *Daily Mirror* (5/11/87) fizzing with the controversy. The Porter was a woman. And she swore profusely. But the real sensation was the shock to the senses. *Macbeth* excited audiences' imaginations in the fantastic atmosphere of supranatural theatricality.

Cheek by Jowl never waste a word (and very occasionally add a few of their own). With an *Othello*, a *Macbeth* or a *Hamlet*, very little is snipped away, so the plays really do speak for themselves, run at a full though not a fulsome length, and never iron out the apparent inconsistencies but confront them head-on. The productions lay the plays bare, stripping them of encrusted expectations, and causing a ripple with the new-found truth.

It seems strange that in a play dominated by the talk of equivocation, it's sometimes thought that things are black and then white, rather than letting the two co-exist. A familiar scenario trundles along the lines of a man bringing tragedy upon himself, with a little help from supernatural forces, which thankfully has the positive consequence of ushering in the new order with a young, fresh-faced Malcolm crossing the border from gloriously stable England, bringing with him lots of milk imagery. With the hindsight of Cheek by Jowl's startling production which exposed the ironic reversals, the dramatic ironies, the austerity of the play's world where all humanity is painted with the same tainted brush, one wonders if this text had remained unexplored before.

Each character was deeply etched, reaching into the darkest recesses of a multi-faceted humanity. Ross was as calculating as Macduff; Malcolm as ugly as Macbeth. Donnellan is candid about such entertainment value, since entertainment reaches beyond the cheap thrills of an ITV game-show:

'I'm sure that the Crucifixion was entertaining. I'm sure the crowd found it interesting or stimulating or entertaining to watch someone being tortured for a day. It can obviously be a bad thing; it can also be a very serious thing. The liturgy is a form of entertainment. I'm only interested in a very broad view of entertainment. Lear's sufferings are entertaining, because they involve us and we have a union with him at a very deep level' (*On Directing Shakespeare* ed. Ralph Berry).

Macbeth begins the play consciously trusting in fate:

'If chance will have me King, why chance will crown me
Without my stir'.

Yet the witches, so often a trio of withered hags, have fatally played their part. In Cheek by Jowl's production, they were not three weird sisters played by three performers, but whispered, howled, and hooted by the whole cast, the staggering reverberations of Macbeth's imagination ('look how our partner's rapt'). Subconsciously, his ambitions were being stirred by his own fantasies. Yet it's misguided human action that finally pricks him to act.

Malcolm is proclaimed heir by Duncan, a literally blind King in Cheek by Jowl's production – his darkness, where he trusted tangible appearances as he traced the features of his kinsmen by placing his hands upon their faces yet was blind to the innermost thoughts of those masks, was a paradoxical eye-opener for the audience. Historically, and the playwright would have been aware of this, it was odd to give Malcolm the royal seal of approval, since Scottish kingship was not hereditary but usually due to him who deserved it most – it's Macbeth, after all, who's just been proclaimed the hero of the battle. The niceties of Dark Age Scottish power-broking weren't the foremost concerns of Cheek by Jowl. Yet the same point of ineptitude and political miscalculation was made apparent since Malcolm was clearly unsuited for kingship. It wasn't only because of his youth or his virginity in a sexually highly-charged environment; it was his disgusting personality: a manic obsessive, with an excruciating stammer, cropped crew-cut hair and spectacled crazed eyes in Timothy Walker's dangerous performance. 'I saw Declan and Nick's production of *Macbeth* in Finland when we were on tour with *Twelfth Night*,' explains Walker:

> 'That Malcolm wasn't remotely like mine, but I wasn't conscious of doing anything different. The reason I stammered was because Declan had perceived that at that stage, after *Twelfth Night* and *The Cid*, I needed to be brought out of myself, to be released as an actor. So he suggested that I do it – it stuck and meant something because it was integrated into the rest of the character. If you commit to the imagination, which is a mysterious and anarchic muscle, you don't know what you're going to end up with'.

The vivid pictures of Walker's characterisations don't just show the extreme torture of social misfits but are indicative of the society of the plays which are made up of those grotesques.

Why the audience became so gripped by the action was not just because of the performances. The production required an active participation. There was no stage blood, for example, simply scrapings on a violin. So the audience became implicated as it imaginatively created blood. All was mimed in the production. Lady Macbeth's rapid application of imaginary rouge, lipstick and mascara to greet Duncan, were prefigurative of her later sleep-walking obsession to remove all of that with cold-cream:

> 'The visual motives of washing and touching sustain an urgent narrative landscape linking the magic of kingship to the cleansing of conscience and guilt' (Michael Ratcliffe *Observer* 8/11/87 Winchester Theatre Royal).

Exposed in Ormerod's murky, sparse setting, slaughter and murder were terrifying – not because of their physical depiction, but because our imaginations ran riot. Macbeth lives in a 'restless

ecstasy', which seemed to be the main phrase of Cheek by Jowl's production, characters and audience alike thrilled by the anxiety and compelled by the fear.

Macbeth has got to do things 'quickly' before he registers the imaginative horror, and Cheek by Jowl's overlapping of scenes and interweaving of action to draw attention to the ironies kept the momentum licking along. Duncan Duff – who was appearing in his first Cheek by Jowl production, playing his trumpet as armies advanced, as well as a whole host of characters – believes this approach to be part of an overall philosophy:

> 'With Declan, the imagination is crucial and central to theatrical experience. That's what really motivates the actor and performance. It's not tangible, but it is the most solid thing. Working with Declan is about exercising the imagination so that you create what you're saying as though it's never been said before.
>
> 'There's also the idea that the performance begins with a pulse of energy, right at its very beginning, which flows through to the end – it's something outside of us which we're carrying throughout the play. Hence all the actors are kept

on stage, rather than going outside of the play into the dressing room. You can't pick up that energy when making a later entrance if you've been having a game of cards in the green room'. Things 'must be acted, ere they may be scann'd'.

In Cheek by Jowl's production, the world was thuggishly brutal from start to finish. It was the same soldiers who chanted 'Sco'land! Sco'land!' at the beginning – delighting in the reports of enemies being 'unseamed from the nave to the chops' – who severed Macbeth's head from his corpse at the end, kicking it over the battlements like a football. It was all very nasty. But it was all in the mind. Eric Shorter was left 'feeling quite queasy' (*Daily Telegraph* 18/11/87 Donmar Warehouse).

It's sometimes not the techniques Cheek by Jowl employ which are new. It's usually their application which strike an audience as innovative. There have probably been countless casts humming and chanting and whistling and hooting to create atmospheric effects. But rarely are they as effective as the shrieks, howls, low murmuring and the cry of a naked new born babe which the *Macbeth* cast created. Ormerod's bare stage of a wooden planked floor not only contained the action but acted as a literal sounding board itself: the irregular sinister shuffles which developed into the black-booted, heavy steps of an army as Birnam Wood came to Dunsinane, the ensemble walking on the spot all along the back of the stage, was more spine-tingling than any motley band of Dad's Army looka-likes scurrying around in hollow treetrunks could ever be. In the mind's eye a sinister army approached. Ormerod's bare stages exist, paradoxically, so that the production can be littered with richer images:

'Having made that decision, you can do things so freely. You can have people drumming their fingers on the stage for rain, or Macbeth or Banquo having been killed just walking off. Audiences will totally and quite happily accept that, because something's being demanded of them which values their involvement in the production',

says Ormerod.

It was a dark world, as much of the audience's own creating as the company's, 'humanity's black collective shadow' (as the quotation from C. G. Jung in the programme indicated). Nick Kidd and Ormerod's lighting design frequently cast real shadows, such as behind the advancing wood, or of the Macbeths at their ominous coronation. The costume of black tops with faint, dark green tartan trousers gave a uniform menace.

Donnellan talked in interviews at the time of the unease of the rehearsal process, where nightmares dogged the company as they unsuccessfully tried to relax from a fetid day of exploration. But what gave some audience members nightmares was the apparent frivolity of the production.

They didn't like Lady Macbeth teasingly chucking imaginary bread rolls at the coronation supper guests to divert their attention from the distracted Macbeth, obsessed with Banquo's ghost. There was a pathos in her sadly watching her husband pick at the remnants of the food once the guests had departed. Here was a devoted couple, ravishing each other as they indulged in a foreplay plotting of Banquo's murder, but to be driven apart by the very seediness of their action. Lady Macbeth's subsequent: 'How now my Lord! Why do you sleep alone?' was a painful entreaty. The potency which turned into impotency may have upset some. The fact that royalty might have foodfights probably upset others. But what really shocked was the word 'fuck'.

Anne White as the Porter gave a controversial run-down of the latest insider-dealing exposés, and Edwina Curry cock-ups within the NHS, much as the Jacobean Porter would have improvised his role, dislocating the audience's expectations after a bloody night of murder. School-teachers were content to take their pupils to see a play about cold-blooded butchery, including killing children. But they were less happy by the use of a word to be heard every day in the playgrounds of even a convent school:

'Convent head Sister Mary Andrew has condemned a Shakespeare production for its "salacious interpretation" and crude and vulgar script. Sister Andrew took 60 young girls from the Towers, Upper Beeding, to a matinée performance of *Macbeth* at the University of Sussex, Gardner Centre.

'She said she was horrified that her pupils, some as young as 12, were submitted to foul language and sexually explicit scenes without having had any previous warning of the play's interpretation. "If the play had been a film it would have had an X certificate and we would have known not to go," she said. "The children were most upset by it and to allow such a thing is absolutely disgraceful" ' (*Adur Herald* 30/10/87).

It is peculiar that minor aberrations from a generally sick play can cause such moral indignity. But it's not something at which Cheek by Jowl would scoff. On publicity for the subsequent productions of *A Family Affair*, *The Tempest* and *Philoctetes*, Cheek by Jowl felt it expedient to state: 'These productions are not recommended for anyone under 16'. Donnellan regretted the necessity:

'We have to protect ourselves. Shakespeare's not at all educational. He celebrates life in all its filth and dirt. It's not about making young people model members of society. I love to see the theatre full of young people, but as long as they come as a sort of adult, sexy exercise. The decision to put that Under 16 warning on the publicity was not taken lightly. I just think it's extraordinary that you have to end up saying that these plays are about life in all its forms' (*Plays International* November 1988).

Anne White remembers the excitement of play-ing, and the antipathy towards, her Porter:

'It sent people out of the theatre, I can tell you. Once I got heckled at Wakefield's Theatre Royal. A man got up just as I came to the end of my speech, and said: "Excuse me, but is this language absolutely necessary?". I'd never been heckled before, so it was a bit of a fright for me, and I thought: "What do I say?". I stalled for time: "I canny hear you". And I marched to the edge of the stage and I looked out: "Language? Language? I'm the fucking Porter!". Wow! He left the theatre and a huge ripple went through the auditorium. Wonderful'.

Timothy Walker identifies the culprit behind the idea of the Porter's first words:

'Nick Ormerod is as much a part of the rehearsal process as the director or any of the actors, and in the same way that Declan draws energy and ideas from the actors for the production, so Nick does for the design. Although notoriously silent, he is very outspoken when he chooses, and has been responsible for some of the more outrageous aspects of productions. For instance, it was his idea that the Porter in *Macbeth*, played as a foul-mouthed bag-woman, should start her speech with an explosive "Fuck off!" ' (from *Potent Art*, unpublished article).

Ultimately, Anne White's Porter in the context of the play was about as shocking as seeing Hamlet in his underpants.

t was only going to be a matter of time before Cheek by Jowl attacked *Hamlet* – a confrontation, one expected, that would unleash hidden invention and push theatrical boundaries [. . .] But the strongly subdued and ritualistic beginning, heightened by the cramped court tableaux struck on Nick Ormerod's raised platform on stage, has a distancing effect that Declan Donnellan's very precise, but hardly inspired, direction never shakes off (James Christopher *Time Out* 28/11/90 Lyric Hammersmith)

It is a pity that the one play that Cheek by Jowl enthusiasts had been eagerly anticipating was disappointing to many – perhaps because everyone was expecting too much, including Declan Donnellan. In a number of interviews towards the end of the eighties, he had been stressing the inevitability that Cheek by Jowl would one day tackle *Hamlet*, like a supreme test of Shakespearian theatrical maturity, and how he would prefer to have a year to rehearse and live within the play with a group of special actors. In the event, he had six weeks, and many felt that some in the cast weren't particularly special.

You could see the thoughts and feelings in particular moments and ideas, and some of the performances were fascinating. Ormerod's little stage in the middle of the main stage was a neat device, enabling scenes to rapidly overlap each other as the next scene began on the main stage's floor while the previous one was coming to an end on the small stage in the middle – at three and a half hours, the virtually uncut text should have seemed to whizz along. Ormerod's stage on stage also encouraged the production decision to open the performance with Daniel Thorndike's Player King, and his group of startled players, calmly pronouncing:

'For us and for our tragedy
Here stooping to your clemency
We beg your hearing patiently'.
Like Hamlet, some wondered, 'Is this a prologue, or the posy of a ring?'.

That Thorndike then quickly appeared as the Ghost (and interestingly one which Horatio, Marcellus and Barnardo weren't frightened by) gave us the impression that it was old King Hamlet who had set up this theatrical revenge, that the whole play was within a framework, and we were watching characters watching characters. Everyone was implicated in eavesdropping behind an arras. That so much could come from so little, is typical of Ormerod's piercing appreciation. But without the wild simplicity one has come to expect from every Cheek by Jowl performer on stage, the set's neutral greyness (despite a huge cloth of crimson draped from the flies for the closet scene, and the true blue costume of Peter Moreton's baby-faced Fortinbras) began to tire the eye. And by choosing to light the performance in appropriate murkiness, the look of the production relied too much on the emerging characters to provide the brightness and colour.

There is an argument that says Cheek by Jowl's *Hamlet* was a kind of pure theatre. There are populist presenters of the classics, Cheek by Jowl being a prime example, whose productions are close to a theatrical neo-classicism, a renaissance, in that they look to the crude purity of the past, before theatre became literature, one which favours the meticulous, pared down classics in a new stage language and form: Theatre of the Heart. 'Heart' does not mean essence or soul (so it's not an absolute) but implies an organic regeneration of the play, constantly growing through practitioners' and audiences' imaginations. Donnellan's friend, contemporary and colleague at the National Theatre, the director Deborah Warner, interviewed by Michael Ignatieff on BBC2's *Late Show* (28/11/89) appreciated that classics are 'great expressions of the human heart'; and she felt that new writing was 'not taking on the possibilities of theatre' (she was, presumably, exempting Donnellan's *Lady Betty*).

Yet *Hamlet* seemed to be underachieved. Perhaps it was the victim of circumstance, too bland in its politics at a time when British interest had been invigorated again by the spectacular ousting of a Prime Minister, a possible interpretation which we were inadvertently encouraged to hope for since Timothy Walker's Hamlet visage on the cover of the programme bore an uncanny resemblance to Mrs Thatcher. Whatever the cause, the effect on critical response was only really detrimental in London. And despite those poor press reports, *Hamlet* still managed to clock up 75% at the Lyric Hammersmith's box office, thanks in part to Ruth Ingledow's blitzing poster campaign, and maybe because there was at least something in the production for everyone to enjoy.

After the feature of music and movement in *Lady Betty* and *Sara*, *Hamlet* seemed to be lacking the essential Gibson-Cunneen input. Gibson points out that she

'did a lot of work on the Court, a lot of high Renaissance dance, because the clothes were like that. Declan sees something and turns around the way you look at it. If it's a classic, which is bigger than everybody, people are aware that it's been undone. Yet it's not as if people were running around in PVC and black plastic bags. *Hamlet* looked as though it was traditional; but it wasn't'.

Apart from drummed and counter-tenor sung interludes, Cunneen's music only seemed to have a dramatic effect when it changed the atmosphere before the grave-diggers' scene. However, Cunneen argues that the music in the production which an audience sees doesn't reveal the extent to which music helped create that production in rehearsal:

'With *Hamlet* we had a separate room downstairs where we used to bang drums and really annoy everyone in the whole building. Sometimes that can be quite good. Often they can be working in one room on a scene, and we'll be in another space working on some music – possibly for it, which we're going to put together afterwards – and the process of the music floating up the stairs and filtering into the rehearsal room actually changes and feeds into what's going on in there'.

Outside London, *Hamlet* was greeted more positively. And abroad, the production was a great success. Dan Furst who reviewed and interviewed the company for a number of press reports in Japan, sends this previously unpublished (abridged) article from the ancient city of Kyoto:

'CHEEK BY JOWL SHOCK: or Just When Japan Thought It Was Safe To Go In The Theatre.

Cheek by Jowl's worldwide audience has grown steadily ever since the company started ten years ago, and now includes thousands of Japanese who saw Cheek by Jowl's *Hamlet* when it played to great acclaim last year in Tokyo and Kyoto under the auspices of the UK 90 arts festival. Most of the Japanese were deeply impressed. Some were stunned. Some were shocked.

The English word 'shock' – pronounced *shokku* here – entered the Japanese vocabulary decades ago. It connotes a surprise so massive and disorienting that it forces an adjustment to new perceptions and realities, and a recognition that the thing the Japanese seem to fear more than anything – *change!* – can no longer be avoided or ignored.

The Japanese who saw their *Hamlet* last year, even those who know the play well, had their images and expectations of Shakespeare knocked out of the usual shelves and boxes, and are still adjusting their estimates of who and what Shakespeare is, and how he ought to be done.

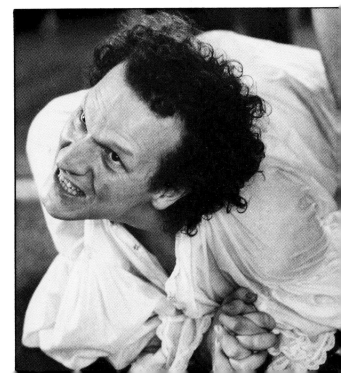

Japan was ripe for shock, for few Japanese had ever imagined that Shakespeare by a British company could be fresh, exciting, and even – astoundingly – fun.

It was no wonder that the Japanese, whose theatre has always suffered from a pronounced hardening of the artistries that even its most daring and vibrant new theatre forms have tended to calcify rapidly into a rigor artis of rules and conventions, have tended to regard Shakespeare as a kind of English kabuki: elaborately set and costumed, formally paced and posed, declaimed in stately measures by severe masters in togas and pumpkin pants. This image of Shakespeare as the archon of British tradition has been reinforced by London companies who have toured Japan since the war in productions that have represented, until very recently, the safest and most conservative stream of British theatre style.

Then Cheek by Jowl arrived, and suddenly something was rockin' in the state of Denmark. Timothy Walker's Prince was no merely melancholy Dane, and Natasha Parry's majestic Gertrude was a stunning revelation in a land where mature women are often played by slightly built men in grey wigs and falsettos. Every actor was consistently alert and engaged that the stage became a virtual cloud chamber of whizzing impulses. Many of the Japanese got to see a real ensemble play for the first time.

It will take Japan a while to hoist all this aboard – but then the pace of life and art is picking up, even in Kyoto. The main thing people here want to know about Cheek by Jowl is: when will they be here again? And the answer everyone wants is: soon; as soon as possible' (2/4/91).

You can only marvel at the panegyrics of a Japanese commentator – and this after Bogdanov and Pennington's ESC *Wars of the Roses* had preceded Cheek by Jowl by a couple of years, and the National Theatre's *King Lear* and *Richard III* had immediately preceded *Hamlet* at Tokyo's Globe Theatre. The effect on the Japanese was even shared by the briefly incumbent British Arts Minister, David Mellor, who was in Japan for the UK 90 festival, and saw his first Cheek by Jowl production on foreign soil:

'I loved the performance. It had zest and real distinction. I was proud of what they did for Shakespeare and for Britain that night'.

Audiences in Greece were similarly impressed. Paris Tacopoulos, seeing Cheek by Jowl's *Hamlet* for a second time at Athens College Theatre (braving the student riots which were sweeping the capital at the time) reported that it was:

'One of the best I have seen, both as an "anarchist" Hamlet and as a "conservative" totality' (*Politika Themata* 18/1/91).

As Cheek by Jowl had so often experienced before, the production changed its whole perspective in a foreign touring environment.

One thing that didn't change was the reception to Timothy Walker's demented Hamlet which was a fascinating character study. He teased Ophelia with 'Get thee to a nunnery', a genuinely affectionate mock at first; once he realises that their kittenish behaviour is being overheard by Polonius and Claudius, the words became venomously real. The first reaction was a modern, preposterous suggestion, the implication being that they had had sex in the past; the second that of a neurotic. She hit out at him wildly; he responded with the *sotto voce* of one soberly sane or nuttily possessed. Walker's Hamlet dropped his trousers to Polonius and blew raspberries at him (contrasting with the proper decorum observed by Polonius' well-brought-up children) a state of undress that Walker remained in for much of the production – Mark Rylance for the RSC in 1989–1990 had merely stripped to his pyjamas; Walker was in his Y-fronts. Ros Asquith observed that Walker:

'Perfectly combines scholar, artist and abandoned child' (*City Limits* 29/11/90 Lyric Hammersmith).

Jeremy Kingston, who felt that Cheek by Jowl had 'come a cropper' with their *Hamlet*, did find some of the readings of Walker's performance appealing:

'In the "too, too solid flesh" soliloquy, Walker invests his second "God!" with such sudden doubt that we glimpse the wildness of fear in a single word' (*Times* 23/11/90 Lyric Hammersmith).

Cathryn Bradshaw's Ophelia was surprisingly sexy, especially since Peter Needham's Polonius

was so stern (no buffoonery from Polonius in this eerily humourless performance). Ophelia giggled with Hamlet, engaged in a sexual frisson with Laertes, and – once she'd been rejected by Hamlet, compounded by the murder of her father – madly flung herself at a distraught Claudius, provocatively humping his midriff.

The choices in casting did provide clever implications for the play. Scott Cherry's young Claudius, scarcely older than Walker, was obviously attractive to the much older Gertrude (the distinguished Natasha Parry) and thus resented by Hamlet who felt both rejected by his mother and protective of her. Claudius wasn't a man happy in power, increasingly giving an unsure delivery of his public statements, crumbling into cowardice after his initial sound politicking of having a wedding so soon after a funeral so that Denmark would look strong to foreign aggressors. But in his opening oration, he knelt to Hamlet to beg him to stay in Elsinore, which humiliated Hamlet publicly, but also showed a new King feeling threatened in his new robes of power.

Despite the individual performances, some people did feel that in general the production was surprisingly weak. Depending on your point of view, it was either austere, typically pared down, measured and considered (and probably enlightening if you'd never seen a Cheek by Jowl production before) – or it was dull, boring and unexpectedly drab (especially if you knew Cheek by Jowl's work well). But Robert Hewison was able to appreciate both points of view and reconcile them as a positive virtue:

'Declan Donnellan's production for Cheek by Jowl at the Lyric, Hammersmith, is the most austere I have seen. But it is all the more dramatic for putting aside the theatrical effects for which his company is usually celebrated' (*Sunday Times* 25/11/90).

Perhaps Cheek by Jowl's *Macbeth* had exhausted their exploration of tragedy as an act of the human imagination. Certainly, by contrast, *Hamlet* was a less imaginative production, though an *Independent* review from the Cambridge Arts Theatre performances still regarded Elsinore as 'a nightmare of neurotic make-believe' (Adrian Poole 20/9/90). As the houselights dimmed at the end of the performance, Duncan Duff's Horatio turned to the audience with a hopeless shrug,

'as if to suggest that the decimation of the Danish court is simply an Absurdist fiction' (Michael Billington *Guardian* 22/11/90 Lyric Hammersmith).

Cheek by Jowl's *Hamlet* continued to demonstrate that this is a company committed to theatricality.

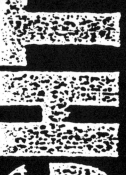

THOUGHT IS FREE

ROMANCE

he zippy narrative, frequent changes of location and plethora of characters make it a playground for drama-skills, and this is what Cheek by Jowl demonstrate [. . .] They present one of those before-your-very-eyes nothing-up-our-sleeves exercises in theatricality (Tom Lubbock *Plays & Players* **March 1985 Donmar Warehouse**)

'Imagine', and then theatre is accomplished. In the worlds of Romance, bizarre happenings and soul-searching journeys grip an audience's imagination when the story-telling and the spiritual self-discovery take on a kind of magical realism. 'Imagine' was repeated by each of the seven performers in turn in *Pericles*, Cheek by Jowl's fourth production, and it constituted the key-word of their first decade. As early as 1984, *Pericles* was, in effect, the summation of an unwritten constitution: celebrating the magic of theatre, the art of story-telling, the richness of constant discovery. Not until their second (and so far last) Romance, *The Tempest* in 1988, did Cheek by Jowl so totally reflect upon itself. And by the time that *The Tempest* was in

rehearsal, Cheek by Jowl had grown in such confidence that no-one needed to be told to 'Imagine' any more; it just happened.

The word 'Imagine' in *Pericles* comes from the narrator Gower's Act III speech, as Shakespeare's play shifts focus, time and place. The part of the narrator was shared amongst the whole company, their style of story-telling such that they were to become the subject of their own narrative, the audience their object. The relationship with the audience had already been established as bare footed actors greeted and chatted to the audience as they arrived, just as they had pressed sweets into the palms of unsuspecting children before the performance of *Vanity Fair*.

Donnellan describes this relationship in a Cheek by Jowl production:

'The emphasis is on the actor and their imagina tions. You cannot define theatre, but I do feel that its supreme moment occurs when the actor's and the audience's imagination meet and something is born between them, and that's why it's import ant that theatre is live. It's to do with the actor and the audience having some sort of imaginative baby. There's always something very exciting and it can be a little frightening, when you have that degree of trust and faith together. I think that you can transcend the poverty of the flesh through the glory of the spirit. It can be the most moving experience, when you collectively sus pend your disbelief. You can see the most poor theatre company working under dreadful circum stances in a destitute city like Bucharest, and you can have an absolutely wonderful theatre experi ence, if the actors and the audience are com pletely wrapped up'.

The theatrical magic in Cheek by Jowl's *Pericles* demonstrated a fearless deconstruction of received notions of Shakespeare in passing, and an exhilarat ing reconstruction of Shakespeare's play. *Pericles* is a play which notoriously confounds the editors and publishers who seek order from chaotic textual material. Through recreation a dead text can be demystified. The actors' performances were liberat ing since they showed the art of the possible.

The production wasn't anecdotally dressed like the comedies of *A Midsummer Night's Dream* or

Twelfth Night, and had few props with most things mimed. 'Using mime freed us to mix periods,' Ormerod recalls,

> 'which we were also able to do because the performers had completely neutral clothes. So we were able to set the brothel scene in a modern brothel with a ghetto-blaster. Other scenes were set in a period which seemed to apply. It was a complete mixture of styles'.

Ormerod's design was far from harsh, allowing for a richness in the production as a whole. The light-blue pyjama costumes (and a Mediterranean slate-blue of the sea was the dominant colour of the set, with bleached, turquoise, wooden screens too) might have placed a constricting uniformity upon the performers, had they not explored the freedom of their thoughts and acting impulses. The costumes had a deliberate neutrality from which anything could be born, the actors' performances alone adorning the production.

Two boxes (made from wooden planks, with rope handles) served as a brothel bed, coffin, port, throne, ship, and Diana's chapel. And the rest of the stage picture was made up of wooden frames which held the musical and percussive instruments within – metal discs, gongs, tubular bells, bamboo shafts, a tin trumpet, the cassette player (which played classical pop muzak), a flute and two thunder sheets (old-fashioned theatre props) for music and for sound effects. All the musical effects contributed to the story of eighteen years travel and adventure which *Pericles* describes: the time and the rhythm; the emotions and the landscapes. Robert Page, seeing *Pericles* at London's Donmar Warehouse, described the effects of the music thus:

> 'The healing, harmonious power of music accompanying all the elemental rhythms of marriage, birth and death, and echoing the transcendental forces of redemption and restitution' (*Times* 15/1/85).

It might all sound as though it was a bit twee, a bit precious, or whimsical, even high-falutin. But Cheek by Jowl never lose a sense of fun. *Pericles* was:

> 'A scenic game rich in ideas, impregnated with a burlesque' (Lorenzo Lopez Sancho *ABC* 17/9/84 Valladolid, Spain).

Just as Ormerod's large, podgy-faced, Arabic Madonna hung high above the action, her arms outstretched in an ambiguously engulfing embrace, the impossible happenings were treated with a delicate irony too:

> 'This excellent company's informal style [...] hits off perfectly the play's combination of self-parody, naive wonder, and where nececessary, deep emotion [...] this is play-making of a complex simplicity that is welcome and very rare' (Tom Vaughan, *Morning Star* 24/1/85 Donmar Warehouse).

However, Marsha Pomerantz was very disappointed when seeing *Pericles* at the Gerard Behar Centre in the Jerusalem Festival during Cheek by Jowl's first official trip abroad:

> 'However ironic the approach, it is never quite caustic enough, and we are left squirming in syrup' (*Jerusalem Post* 13/6/84).

And not everyone agreed that it was good or original. Steve Grant from *Time Out* felt that:

> 'There are certain clichés of fringe-group approaches to the classics (notably a hideous slow motion sequence and the token homage to the Shared Experience school of narrative orchestration)' (17/1/85 Donmar Warehouse).

Duncan Bell remembers the mixed feelings he had about that slo-mo acting:

> 'When we did *Pericles*, we did an Olympics, miming slow-motion running, a horse race, firing a bow and arrow. I thought: "What the hell is this?". Sometimes you would find yourself in the middle of a show doing slow-motion archery and wonder: "Why is this my life?". You often wondered how you got away with it. I guess it was taken on trust. People might come backstage afterwards and say it was stupid – but they would say that it was engaging. There's always a resistance to simplicity from both actors and audiences. It takes a perverse courage to say: "It's as simple as this". Sometimes it's difficult to believe, even after a Laurence Olivier Award'.

Olivier Awards or not, it's the wildness of the images making fresh sense of the text that so many people find rewarding. The dynamism of a Shakespeare romance gives Cheek by Jowl a special momentum.

t gripped the audience, many among whom were young people for whom Shakespeare might be in danger of becoming an academic text to be tolerated till the examinations are over. People reacted; they laughed; they held their breath; they wanted the play to go on. The stage expanded till it included the hall [...] The magic was on (Asad Latif *Business Times* 23/1/89 Victoria Theatre Singapore)

In Britain, *The Tempest* was an extraordinary indulgence in Cheek by Jowlery, a solipsistic pursuit of theatricality, using whatever means seemed appropriate at particular moments in the play to highlight what *The Tempest* meant to this inexhaustibly investigative company. A young, arrogant director, Prospero, on the verge of a nervous breakdown, dragooning his cast into enacting his insane conceptualisations; they responding to his manic obsession through generous improvisation; a brash vaudeville double-act of Trinculo and Stephano with their sequinned bowler-hats, their sparkling red-trimmed waistcoats, their gaudy patched trousers and springy baseball boots, all signalling the crass cult of the individual – their simplistic notions of freedom and gulling an articulate but naive Caliban (singing 'There's no such thing as Society!' after Mrs Thatcher's catchphrase of the day, and à la Lloyd Webber):

'a dark view of the world in which the illusion of freedom is easily available on tick, like bread and circuses to keep the simple in their place' (Michael Ratcliffe *Observer* 13/11/88 Towngate Theatre Basildon).

By being receptive to all sorts of art forms, Cheek by Jowl make their own art potent.

In Eastern Europe, *The Tempest* was a dangerous cry for freedom from the shackles of entrenched Stalinism, freely screamed from the stage with revolutionary zeal. It wasn't the production which changed radically as it visited contrasting nations throughout the world. It was the spirit in which it was received which did. In the pre-Velvet Revolution days of Czechoslovakia, audiences were stunned as the foreign performers descended from the stage to chat to them because any conference with Western aliens had to be reported to the police within twenty-four hours. And in Romania, 'Hi-day freedom' upset Politburo members but thrilled the 2,000-packed auditorium (crammed three-abreast in the aisles) since '*Haide*' means 'Let's go for it!'.

The Tempest is thus not only an abstract tinkering with art for art's sake; it's a play parading the atrocious authoritarianism of political oppression. Cheek by Jowl's travel abroad has prepared them for the joy with which their productions are received, as they glimpse the pros and cons of contrasting cultures. In Poland with *Twelfth Night* in 1987, they couldn't photocopy scripts for a workshop since photocopier machines were prohibited to curtail the spread of *samizdat* publications. In Romania with *The Tempest* and *Philoctetes* in 1988, they would run their hotel room taps while talking; note down names and addresses silently rather than speak them out loud; and Donnellan would switch from giving a talk in English to French, frustrated that the interpreter was being economical with his truth. 'Romania was unforgettable,' says Timothy Walker:

'The moment when we came to the Masque and the actors spiralled out of control and started chanting "Freedom! Hi-day freedom!", it was such an odd position to be in as Prospero because I was in a direct confrontational relationship with that particular audience at that particular time, realising that we'd released something that we hadn't necessarily intended to release through an

act of theatre. It was very peculiar because I, as Prospero, was in a position to decide how long to play the slow hand-clapping and jeering, that had begun after the Masque, and carry on with: "Our revels now are ended" '.

Where we take freedom for granted, we can be more concerned with artistic interpretation than political polemics. *The Tempest* in Britain split the critical reaction – from those who saw Cheek by Jowl at their most experimental and at their exploratory best; to those who derided the monkeying around. Depending on your perspective, it was either deconstruction or reconstruction of the play's themes, vigorously shaking the conflicts of power and class, race and imperialism, creativity and nihilism as a series of confrontations. Caliban served Prospero tea as a bolshy butler, scruffily attired in his ill-fitting colonial white waiter-garb, not tamed enough to prevent him throwing the tea in his master's face (a powerful characterisation in Duncan

Duff's intelligent performance). An eighteenth century fop, Ferdinand (Lloyd Owen) strutted his pouting-rouged aristocrat until stripped of his powder-puff pretension on the island. Paddy Cunneen composed a rap of Ariel's song for Ferdinand 'because it seemed like a pop video'. Cunneen's music was extraordinary throughout, as eclectic as the production:

'It seemed to me from what Declan was saying, that the idea for the metaphor of Prospero's magic was going to be theatre. Once you've got that; once you're that free, you can chuck in anything and it should work. It's like the Stravinsky thing: that once you've found the rules for doing something then you are completely free. (Freedom without rules is terrifying.)

'You have to beg the audience's indulgence, using the music in a way which says to them: "You've got to come along with us on this. We're suggesting something; we are not going to do it

for you; we are inviting your participation because we haven't got a full orchestra so one clarinet represents all the brass you've ever heard" '.

Even more than the music, the casting seemed a haphazard affair too, but again there were rules to this freedom. Prospero, adopting the role of the ship's Master in scene one, chucked costumes at his actors in the initial improvisation, the actors eagerly taking on the role they were thrust into (a cap for a 'Boatswain') appeasing his artistic wrath, and giving him the creative life-line when his own ideas halted: 'If by your art, my dearest *father*' from a Miranda, creating a role for Prospero, and a relationship, within his spontaneous world. This free-roaming, generous improvisation emerged from the initial warming-up exercises each evening, the playing of instruments (including a piano on stage) and chatting to the audience as they arrived:

'At one point, the two lovers, Ferdinand and Miranda, were at the lower steps of the auditorium hobnobbing with the audience. The spotlight focused on the romantic pair as well as the audience clustered around them. Thus, the audience was caught in the act of being an audience' (Utih *New Sunday Times* 5/2/89 Dewan Bandaraya, Kuala Lumpur).

There was an androgynous Ariel from Peter Darling. And Anne White was the Queen of Naples ('Full fathom five thy fair Queen lies') surrounded by an all-male retinue. The actors' imaginations were fired by fresh ideas and by contrasting venues, as Timothy Walker recorded in Perth, Australia:

'Tonight, we will re-invent *The Tempest*, in an open space like an Elizabethan courtyard. There are peacocks, overhanging vines, our wild array of costumes and props; we can hear Brook's *Carmen* warming up nearby – an eclectic fusion in a Festival for the Arts. But then Prospero – a magician, stained with grief, able to transform and new create himself and others, as his soul prompts it, through the magic of theatre – inhabits such an island, where there are strange noises, ship-wrecked people whose garments though drenched in the sea are fresher than before, whose souls are possessed with guilt. The stimulus of this new and magical setting is in my

imagination and is no different from the stimulus Prospero feels on encountering each new and strange moment as it happens in the play: the play influences the way I see its setting and the setting becomes a part of the play. Imagination and reality interpenetrate and the inability clearly to define the parameters is not a confusion but the freedom the creative mind needs if it is to work properly' (from *Potent Art*, unpublished article).

The huge array of costumes from various periods, grabbed from a costume rail and out of the troupe's basket, created a setting of theatrical artifice. With a red velvet curtain in the second half of the play, the stage forms alluded to were deliberately multiple. Amongst additional backstage paraphernalia, the most important was the dressing table with its mirror edged by the light bulbs of show-biz, at which Prospero would slap on increasingly grotesque layers of make-up to become a parody of Olivier's Richard III, or a Dickensian undertaker (shades of Walker's Rispolozhensky creeping in) — all deliberately self-conscious cross-referencing from this tyrannical man of art and artifice. The production was a cleverly thought through 'iconoclastic mish-mash', driving 'every possible Shakespeare sacred cow off the stage' (Mary Amos *The Australian* 8/2/89 New Fortune Theatre Perth). Though Martin Hoyle did worry:

'I have a sneaking suspicion that cleverness for cleverness' sake is the company's besetting sin' (*Financial Times* 20/10/88 Theatre Royal Bury St Edmunds).

Perhaps those who didn't know the play at all might have been a trifle confused.

In Edinburgh in 1988 there had been Frank Dunlop's Japanese import of Ninagawa's production of *The Tempest* which also had an ensemble of actors putting on a play but within the tight framework of Noh Drama. Cheek by Jowl was using any style that seemed to fit. Paddy Cunneen's music was often the essence of the play's magic, sometimes ethereal, sometimes spritely; and he wasn't afraid of the simple impulse to use the appropriately stirring gaucheness of the company hymning 'For Those in Peril on the Sea' as the ship sinks in the opening storm.

In 1988 there were three other major *Tempests* playing in England: with John Wood's Prospero for the RSC, Stratford-upon-Avon; Max von Sydow's at the Old Vic; and Michael Bryant's at the National Theatre. Timothy Walker's was the youngest, and very much against the grain:

'Donnellan's determination would seem to be never to let us think we know the play and never let it drift into mere recital or repetition: every scene and every character has been rethought' (Sheridan Morley *International Herald Tribune* 7/12/88 Donmar Warehouse).

Donnellan's rethinking wasn't arbitrary in a negative sense, since it reflected the vigorous irrationality of a play which isn't strictly linear, or veering between two polarities, but is a romance in that it follows through any imaginative impulse, often surrealistically, bizarrely squaring a circle. 'The more we looked at the play,' explains Donnellan (in *On Directing Shakespeare*),

'the less we believed in the traditional serene image. It had a very noisy title. Prospero we saw as a magician who can transform himself and other people's perceptions of the world. He is obsessed by his power, his rough magic and his art. The narrative line of the play is often crushed under Prospero's erratic creative energy, as, for example, when he aborts the masque. We felt it would be a withering imposition to strangle the play with narrative control, e.g. by setting it in a specific period, on a specific island. We had to find a way to match Shakespeare's outrageous inventiveness and breathtaking disregard for any theatrical tradition' (ed. Ralph Berry).

Hence Prospero's sedate masque for Ferdinand and Miranda became an earthy, romping barn dance.

Keith Bartlett recalls how his comic input as Stephano wasn't always gleefully welcomed:

'In Kuala Lumpur they loved the comedy. In Italy it didn't go down so well. We opened in Taormina

and I came on with the snorkel and the mask and the flippers, to look silly, out of water. And they just looked and thought: "What's funny about that? Yeah, Snorkel. So?" '.

By the end of each performance, the actors were properly relieved, both visually and vocally, when Prospero, the director, declared that 'These revels now are ended'. Ariel – released from flying through the air balletically, or being dragged by Ferdinand as his burden of logs, gliding back for Ferdinand to drag again – demonstrated that he could only jump six inches in the air once released from the spell, again an actor. *The Tempest* was pure Cheek by Jowl because it was full of all the impurities of theatre, following every thought freely thrown up by the actors, director, designer and composer to its wildest extremes. Out of the silliness of playmaking (though never as silly as Donnellan had looked when at the age of sixteen he had played Trinculo in his school-play at St Benedict's, Ealing, with a phallus strapped to his head) came the darker aspects of dangerous creativity. And then in Eastern Europe, this cultural subversion interpretation took on the mantle of political anarchy. 'The thought is free'; a thought which changes as the people from whom it is provoked change.

The sexual and political violence of the play was always at the forefront of the production – the neuroses of Prospero seeking to protect his daughter's virginity; the plotting of insurrection. But, depending on the audience, these themes can be either concrete or abstract. In the concrete mausoleum of late eighties Communist Europe, the politics took on a piercing relevance.

Michael Coveney, in Prague to report on Cheek by Jowl's *Tempest* and *Philoctetes* in March 1989 for the *Financial Times*, recalls a party in the British Embassy where the new Ambassador, the amiable Laurence O'Keefe (an Irishman) laughed a lot about Trinculo's 'Union Jack-assed bottom', enjoying the risqué point about bulldog colonialism. But Coveney feels that Cheek by Jowl's 'sort-of-political versions of the classics' are precisely risqué because they are never risky. However, in Romania, risks were at a premium.

Alec Pattison of the British Council had first met Cheek by Jowl when they presented *A Midsummer Night's Dream* in Kathmandu, Nepal in October 1988. They received a unanimously buoyant reception for their adventurousness with a Shakespeare comedy. In Romania, where Pattison was next posted, he knew of the personal and political risks that all involved in any cultural import would face (not least his own secretary, Aura Ulad, a native Romanian) and the official bad reception that a visiting company would receive from the official media. But he suspected that Cheek by Jowl would have an extraordinary popular appeal.

It took nine months to clear the visit with the Ministry of Culture (the first visit by a British company to Romania since the Manchester Royal Exchange in the 1970's, and eagerly anticipated by those who still remembered the impact of the RSC's Brook/Scofield *King Lear* which came to Romania in the 1960's). They were content to let Shakespeare play their national stage, unaware that it was more than universal poetry, but were dubious, even nervous, of an English company wanting to perform a Greek play, *Philoctetes*. It was during a point in Ceaucescu's iron rule where there was increased resistance to foreign visitors or allowing their own people trips abroad. When Elena Ceaucescu had seen a queue for an American art exhibition in Bucharest, she had immediately demanded its closure, the eager Romanians returning to the food queues, their frozen homes with their power-cuts, their scrabbling around for scraps of clothing, their lack of freedom of movement even within their own country since the public transport facilities were dire.

Culture to the Romanians was a means of escape from a dreadful situation, and the live thrill of the theatre was particularly cherished. Most would even enjoy the moribund productions of traditional plays by the state's national companies; all were to be shocked with excitement by Cheek by Jowl (a different kind of shock from the Japanese's at *Hamlet*). The company brought a freshness and modernity to the staid show-case of Romania's National Theatre. It wasn't that the ideas were necessarily new to Romanians – the British Council and the BBC World Service had done their best to keep people clued up on British and Western culture – but they hadn't actually seen it for a long time. Ultimately, theatre needs to be seen to be believed.

'We'd had reports from Czechoslovakia,' says Pattison, (who was nervous of being interviewed with a tape-recorder, even in his London Spring Street office where he is now Head of Education for the British Council, since his experiences in Romania have left him with a reflexive distrust of any recorded conversation),

'so we knew we were in for an exciting time. We also knew that we had to keep those reports hidden from the Ministry of Culture. After the visit, I learned that the officials in charge were carpeted and threatened with expulsion for having let the productions into the country.

'Romanian theatre was not adventurous at the time. To see this was unbelievable for them. It was a clash between the traditional, government controlled art which they were used to, and the free and lively individualistic Cheek by Jowl. We didn't give it too much pre-publicity because we knew what was coming and we didn't want it to get called off. We were surreptitious. We also wanted as many young people to see it as possible rather than get block bookings from the 23rd of August Factory Workers'.

A 1,300 seat auditorium housed an audience of up to 2,000 a night, so keen were people to witness this rare event. The Party hacks at the front of the stalls didn't smile once – the enthusiasm from the hall was overwhelming. They cheered Caliban; hooted Prospero as he daubed his make-up in his dressing-room 'cell', uncannily a reflection of the Ceaucescu's box opposite the stage (which remained empty with its curtains drawn – the Ceaucescus had apparently only been once to their National Theatre to see a variety show). Far from being the diplomatic ambassadors to promote commercial contracts which people often assume is the sole role of the British Council, Pattison, knowing the mind of his Ambassador, Hugh Arbuthnott, recognised that it was through cultural imports that repression could be combatted, the abnormal existence of the people freed momentarily by showing them a dimension of life which they had long forgotten. Theatre was always an escape for them – but The Tempest was the biggest escape of all.

One man from the audience grabbed Donnellan at the stage door after a performance, thrusting a sculpture into his hands: 'My art for your art', the man muttered modestly. A woman was so overcome by the production that she rushed up on stage after one performance, grabbed an actor and asked him to marry her. Unfortunatly for her, she'd picked upon Charlie Roe, the only married member of the company. But they arranged a rendezvous and he heard her grievances sympathetically.

Anne White playing the Queen of Naples had been likened to Mrs Thatcher in Britain and in the parts of the old Empire where the production toured. In Romania, she played the same matriarchal figure with the same pearls, the same posture, and even the same distinctive walk. The audience were in unbelieving hysterics, not because they too saw the Thatcher factor, but because they were so impressed that White had managed to get their First Lady, Elena Ceaucescu, down to a tee. People in power cut the same figure, it seems; and that power is ephemeral, all in the eye of the beholder.

Any visit by any Western company would have had an effect. That the visit was by Cheek by Jowl with a pair of political plays – politically disturbing for the country's status quo and for the individual – was particularly inspiring for those who saw the productions. All over the world they had resonances peculiar to the particular social environment in which they were performed. What was crucial to Cheek by Jowl's treatment was the way the company recognised that the scripts mix their own worlds in the crucible of an island. In The Tempest, this is reflected in the language and the free thoughts that produce a range of theatrical forms and a hybrid of themes of potentiality.

The stagecraft, which all involved in the production would claim was inspired by the text, was a summation of Cheek by Jowl's theatrical innovation. It influences other theatre practitioners. Joan Bakewell, seeing a Monday night Tempest at the Theatre Royal, Bury St Edmunds, reported that:

'Purists must hate it. But the sheer inventiveness is seeding ideas for theatrical inventiveness in theatres across the country' Sunday Times 16/10/88).

AS YOU LIKE IT OR WHAT YOU WILL

COMEDY

heek by Jowl took you by the scruff of the neck, tickled, prodded and coaxed you into prodigious laughter. And when they let go, they left behind a gift. The gift of making you look afresh, and question the unquestioned, even the classic (Aditi De *Indian Express* 28/2/86 Madras Music Hall)

A Midsummer Night's Dream's tour of the Indian sub-continent was a real hoot. Rarely in Indian play-houses do sporadic trickles of muffled applause break out; but Cheek by Jowl received this curiously positive response. Audiences the world over delighted in the revelations of a play that they thought they knew, the contemporary context feeding the wildness of the actors' imaginations to create vast scenes of unrelenting joy on just a white cloth floor (and against two pieces of the same cloth which hung at the rear of the stage for simple projections of a wood to be cast upon them). In Pakistan, Cheek by Jowl

'introduced Lahore's theatre-goers to a boldness of style and fertility of innovation that will hopefully inspire our own rather staid theatre' (*Pakistan Times* 24/1/86 Alhamra Arts Centre).

Yet for all its verve, *A Midsummer Night's Dream* received a fair amount of criticism for taking liberties with literature; which only goes to show, there's nothing like a bit of modern dress to upset the stuck-in-the-muds. You might say that they have just cause, since so many companies have plastered extraneous gags on top of a play, afraid that no one will find an Elizabethan romp all that funny any more (and too often their self-inflicted comedy does prove a tiresome farce). Forced laughter is rarely satisfying. Cheek by Jowl highlight and open up a play, engaging us in their humour. Yet perhaps because there's no cod-piece prettiness, Cheek by Jowl's Shakespeare comedies have received a knee-jerk condemnation from some quarters.

Critical concerns with the type of anachronistic settings that Shakespeare never seems bothered about, emanate from a sense of literary decorum. By denying a Shakespeare production a contemporary setting at all, such critics ignore that those Renaissance values which they cherish (or rather those that people like E. M. W. Tillyard in *The Elizabethan World Picture* procure) can co-exist with modern evaluations.

A play doesn't need a contemporary setting for an

audience to appreciate that sharing or contrasting of ideas (*A Family Affair* proved a case in point); but it can make the process of recognising aspects of those plays in ourselves (rather than forcing ourselves arrogantly into those plays) more immediate. The past isn't being judged on the terms of our own times; it's the present which has a fresh light thrown upon it by rediscovering aspects of the past — less through intellectual game-playing and more by theatrical play-making in a Cheek by Jowl production.

One such revelation in Cheek by Jowl's *Midsummer Night's Dream* was that the wood, where the Night is spent, is a dangerous place, unknown to the lovers except in their imaginations, and is not some Elizabethan ideal of a playground for love. So, it sometimes became a jungle, the actors buzzing and hooting.

Saskia Reeves, still besotted by her *Midsummer Night's Dream* experience as Hermia, vividly remembers the imaginative ideas of that production:

'What Declan brings to rehearsal is his personality. It's as if sparks fly out of his head sometimes. In *A Midsummer Night's Dream*, Theseus is angry with Hermia because she's cavorting with somebody she shouldn't be. He lists endless gripes – it became like taking her to court. So then the scene took on a legal quality, Theseus becoming a barrister. Hermia was probably at law school herself, she's not stupid. It helps the audience to see more clearly by telling the story. I love the improvisational quality; although we were working with a text, there was a great sense that it was free.

'If Declan is sending a production off in one direction, then Nick takes it even further. So, if you're setting it in modern England, and these Sloaney characters run away, Nick thinks: "Okay. I'll kit them out. I'll give them sleeping-bags and rucksacks". And then we'd take up the idea with loads of things dangling off those rucksacks: "What about pots and pans?" – "We could have flasks" – "We could have cups". You simplify it down – we ended up with a map, a torch, and boots hanging off the rucksacks – and it creates an image you can relate to. That's what they do.

They say: "It's not an old play. It's still about people" '.

Donnellan often claims that 'Shakespeare is Britain's greatest living playwright', and it is his fresh productions which breathe life into texts which have been almost flogged to death with literary criticism and run-of-the-mill productions. *A Midsummer Night's Dream* is so familiar a comedy — read at school, seen on countless school trips – that audiences can become bored with regurgitated comic action. It takes a strong and innovative sense of humour to make us laugh all over again at an old joke, and even more miraculously to discover a new one that has been there all along but which has been passed over by scores of traditional treatments. Together, Donnellan, Ormerod, and the performers achieved this with hilarious results.

Not that the excitement of the company's approach was untamed. There was a care, a painstaking sobriety, rehearsal mayhem tempered by the knowledge that frivolous stage business obscures rather than edifies. Donnellan is a sound judge of the superfluous, cutting out the unnecessary. Sheila Fox recognised that:

'Accessibility is the key: their main aim is to democratise the classics, make them connect with an audience that's running scared of high-church culture' (*City Limits* 21/3/86 Donmar Warehouse).

A Midsummer Night's Dream wasn't cheap and tacky, with instant association to get a quick laugh as a clap-trap for a clap-happy, low-church of silly theatre-goers. The entertainment was far from hollow and the laughter hearty, not superficially giggly. Here was theatre with guts and purpose, not some firework display to make you 'ooh' and 'aah' at the fleeting pretty sparkle, only to be bereft of satisfaction afterwards. Without needing to use any elaborate gadgetry, Ormerod's costume design and a few precisely suggestive props lost none of the passion of a world peopled with self-indulgent, narcissistic lovers. It enhanced the self-recognition for the audience.

The gold-rimmed, circular specs of Saskia Reeves' goofily earnest, short-sighted Hermia, focused the way that the playwright pokes fun at her and Lysander as they excitedly run away to the wood.

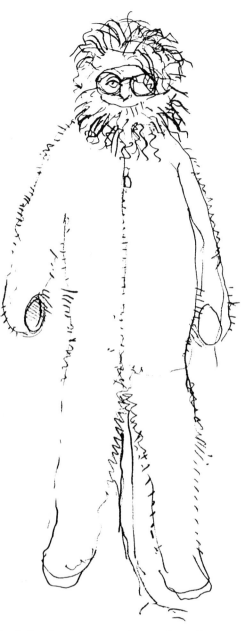

Carrying their rucksacks and bright blue sleeping bags, they jaunted off in their sensible hiking-boot footwear. Visually, we could see that these two, off on a jolly jape, thought that they were the masters of their own destiny, and thus their lack of emotional preparation for their journey was juxtaposed with their hale and hearty organisation of practicalities. Following a kind of middle-class scout's honour to be well-prepared, these characters nonetheless unwittingly exposed their emotional naivety as they spontaneously flirt with danger. Similarly, though by contrast, the stiff, city-suited Demetrius looked uncomfortable, attired in an inappropriate Burberry mac – a touch of John Cleese uptightness in William Chubb's balding, harassed, self-important city-stockbroker performance, embarrassed by the show of affection from a scarved, Husky-wearing Helena.

Theseus and Hippolyta were likened to Prince Charles and Lady Di, with 'clenched Mountbatten-Windsor tones' (Martin Hoyle *Financial Times* 20/3/86 Donmar Warehouse). Oberon and Titania were far more dangerous, shady and sinister in their spirit world. There was a pipe-smoking, woolly jumper-wearing (as woolly as his ideals) Reverend Bottom, with a sychophantic spinster Miss Quince and Miss Flute – the mechanicals merged into a trio for a cloying cosiness as much as for practical touring-company requirements. All were appealing; not because they were familiar stereotypes, but because they were theatrical prototypes.

The world of a selfish South East England was created behind the rumbustious humour, deliberately deflationary as it pricked the self-inflated egos of all (it's the script that doesn't let any of the characters off the hook). This world of contemporary Sloanes and do-gooding reverends was not a tricksy presentation but the consequence of a desire to show a play to a contemporary audience, without the academic footnotes or a strange respect for Great Art clouding our vision of the script. Of course, the kids'll love it: but that's because the intellectual rigour behind the hilarity is constantly invigorating. If in the end we revelled in our laughter, then that sheer pleasure was supremely positive:

'There doesn't exist for man a more effective remedy than laughter, and this is what the group

Cheek by Jowl is proposing: only to laugh. To laugh and laugh as an undeniable vote for life' (Beatriz Iacoviello *Clarin* 23/4/86 Teatro Nacional Brazilia).

Much of the laughter was magical. A bungling Puck would freeze the lovers at a click of a finger or fling them with boundless athleticism through the night. Thus the constant inventiveness and surprise was threatening as one could never predict which way the play would turn (as in a dream, the fantasy always has sinister, nightmarish possibilities). 'Entrancing' was as oft-cited of this production as 'cheeky', the laughter not slapstick-induced but of delight and amazement.

A Midsummer Night's Dream is a play about playing, and the am. dram. theatricals of the mechanicals highlighted the over-committed involvement of those who take it all terribly terribly seriously. Leda Hodgson as Miss Flute would be puffing away at her cigarettes and then warming up with ridiculous breathing exercises in her 'Relax' tee-shirt:

'a type familiar to all amateur groups: the method actress who does a Grotowski warm up before every rehearsal' (Michael Ratcliffe *Observer* 23/3/86 Donmar Warehouse).

Despite the send-up (and it's the playwright's to start with) the play is ultimately a celebration of the humanising and self-awareness that comes from experiencing the extremes of fantasy (and those manifest in the act of playmaking are indicative). It mischievously seems to be a play about love – Mendelssohn's Wedding March (wittily from his *Midsummer Night's Dream* ballet) opened the play, drawing attention to the limitations of entrenched social codes of practice, which Shakespeare then turns topsy-turvy – but there's nothing as compelling for the individual's own self-devotion as unrequited love.

Donnellan had directed *A Midsummer Night's Dream* before at the Arts Educational School. Barbara Matthews saw this production, and she suggests that it was with her goading that Cheek by Jowl chose to mount the play:

'We had just done *Andromache* and *Pericles* and all those other really easy to sell shows! I could see Declan looking at Goethe and I thought to myself that it was about time that I had a show that was easy to sell. I said it was a real pity that we couldn't do *The Dream* – because Declan had had a cast of twenty-four at Arts Ed., which we could never afford (so many fairies they were coming out of his ears). So, he went away, and thought about it, and decided that he would do it'.

Even a cast of ten wasn't enough to satisfy that need for fairies. So, inspired by not having them, the company arrived at a trick whereby the three mechanicals were possessed by spirits. It was grotesque and bizarre, but funny and fresh, the spirited Miss Quince and Miss Flute 'starting to do very indecent things with Mr Bottom', says Ormerod. 'That was something we discovered through poverty,' thinks Donnellan:

'If we'd been able to have the extra six actors we wouldn't have come to that solution. There are certain things which are positive about not having huge resources. But there are certain things which are very limiting'.

The production visited Uruguay, Cheek by Jowl's first visit to the Montevideo Festival (the second came with *Sara* in 1990) where it was as much of a hit as it was in Asia. Researching the event some years on, the Commercial Officer to the British Embassy in Montevideo, Eduardo Pose, states:

'Their production was recognised by all as far the most outstanding on view or seen then for the freshness of their approach and the all-round technical ability of the cast'.

Uruguay is a small country, now without the danger, violence, colour and heat one usually associates romantically with South American countries, such as Brazil, but then a political hot-house. It's so far south that the weather is seasonal: during the April Festival, the weather is like a chilly English Autumn. However, in 1986, there were still heated passions and hatred for the English. Even though *A Midsummer Night's Dream* visited in 1986, the hostility towards the English was extreme, post Falklands War. One Foreign Office source suggests that Cheek by Jowl brought a kind of *détente*, giving a fresh impetus to the restoration of relations between Britain and South America. Perhaps that's claiming too much? But where the appeal of their production could quite forseeably have been met with begrudging approval, it was genuinely generous.

A Midsummer Night's Dream was a rejuvenation of a comic text which proved highly popular, just as with their production of *Twelfth Night*. When Cheek by Jowl were thinking about their tenth anniversary production, it should come as no surprise that an early suggestion to mount a cycle of medieval Mystery Plays was dropped in favour of presenting a Shakespeare comedy, *As You Like It*. In a theatre full of lightweight comedy, it falls upon companies like Cheek by Jowl to provide the heavyweight challenge.

You never know what is enough unless you know what is more than enough [. . .]
The road of excess leads to the palace of wisdom.
Prudence is a rich ugly old maid courted by Incapacity.
He who desires but acts not, breeds pestilence.
The cut worm forgives the plow (William Blake, *The Marriage of Heaven and Hell*)

Quoting 'the road of excess leads to the palace of wisdom' in *Twelfth Night*'s programme was a statement of a Cheek by Jowl philosophy. On a practical level, theatre has the potential to reach far beyond the safety of the orthodox and the unimaginative acceptance of tradition. In exploring what we too easily accept are our limitations, we discover that we not only have the potential, but also the capacity to become richer human beings.

For all the plays Cheek by Jowl produce, this Blake quotation (achieved through allowing the freedom of imagination) can be seen to apply specifically to the misleadingly dubbed minor characters. Cheek by Jowl explore everyone, keen to stress the voices of those marginalised by their culture, giving a privilege to all the characters, not just the leading roles. Through a sense of the carnivalesque as an atmospheric context, a populist expression of creativity, and looking at the weaker voices of the powerless to see their strengths (and delving into the grottiness of the powerful to find their weaknesses) Cheek by Jowl's productions show a wider range, an extra dimension, so that the plays become bigger.

In Cheek by Jowl's *Twelfth Night*, the characters who dominated the audiences' imaginations were not just the Orsinos and Violas, but the unattractively-named Belch and Aguecheek too. Toby Belch was a knight, but a pitiful one, sporting his MCC tie and, by having a betting slip permanently tucked in his top hat's ribbon, an obvious punter on the horses. He read the *Sporting Life* too. You could tell a lot about a character in this production by what they read: Malvolio, *The Sunday People*; Olivia, *Country Life*. But these weren't the be-all and end-all, they were merely guidelines to lead the audience in. Belch also had latent aggression, suddenly provoked into a bottle fight. The comic characters were deeply unsettled and unsettling.

Keith Bartlett, who played Belch, describes how Aden Gillett had a flash of inspiration about Sir Andrew Aguecheek:

'Declan was talking about Aguecheek as being a visitor to the area. He obviously has a fair bit of money. So Aden was saying over a pint in Vauxhall how Aguecheek sounded a bit American. The week before there'd been an *Observer* article about Americans coming over and buying honours. I said: "That's it. Toby Belch can sell you an honour for cash, and that'll give you respectability". And Aden took it from there, suddenly making sense of "I'm a great eater of beef and I believe that does harm to my wit" '.

Each time Gillett's Texan Aguecheek made an entrance he would swagger appropriately. Yet he was compassionate: 'I was adored once too'.

The characters are revealed, as in *A Midsummer Night's Dream*, as vain and pitiful. 'Hold thy peace!',

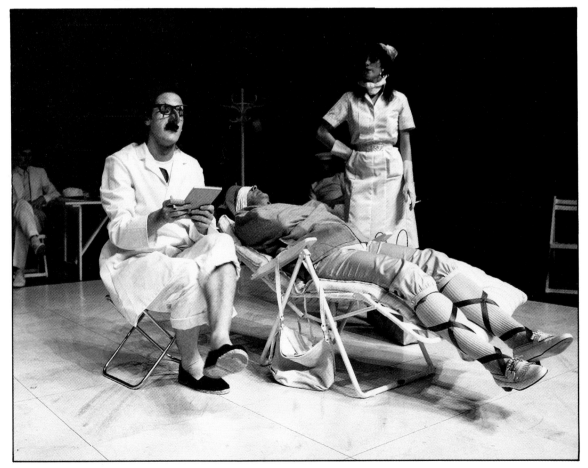

someone cries, and they did, for over a minute, indulging in alcohol-induced self-pity through the still silence, broken only by a self-deluding, tuneless rendition of Sinatra's 'My Way', the pathos of these characters revealed. Joanna MacGregor's music was a major means of expression and communication: Viola played a trumpet; Maria (who also had an American accent, a raunchy Brooklyn one, and smoked cheroots) a saxophone raucously; Toby Belch a guitar; and lots of harmonicas, tom-toms and Latin American instruments thrown in, to accompany a calypso that closed the show.

A sober-suited Malvolio donned the yellow stockings of a safari outfit, thinking pompously that he was out on a dangerous hunt to tame the beast of love. Though he definitely wasn't a sympathetic character, as the legacy of the Victorian tradition often informs the role, there were moments of intimacy. Reading the false love-letter, he cried

joyously, only to be embarrassed that he should be caught doing so in front of an audience (in the theatre) and thus he self-consciously regained his composure. But Malvolio was a sinister threat, all smiles at the end of the play in a jolly show of forgiveness, delivering his 'I'll be revenged on the whole pack of you' as a terrifying aside to the audience.

The characters were deliberately exposed on Ormerod's, spotlit, chequerboard-tiled, square stage. From the ceiling hung a grandfather clock, a guitar, and a ship's wheel. The wheel was lowered at the beginning of the play – as some productions had done before, the shipwreck of Scene Two came first; 'If music be the food' of Scene One, coming second. The dominant colour of the design was white: white table and chairs, panama hats, bandannas and dark sun-glasses. The Duke Orsino was a Royal Navy Commander in white flannels, surrounded by a retinue of sailors. Feste (amalgamated with the part of Fabian to make him feature centrally in the story) was curiously a white-faced clown, with a black cross painted around each eye. This was the end of a foreign Empire for the British, with some of the colonials out on a last fling.

Cheek by Jowl's *Twelfth Night* was the first ever Shakespeare to play in the RSC's Stratford-upon-Avon Swan Theatre. And like subsequent productions of Shakespeare's plays in that theatre, it revelled in its close contact with the audience, with its minimalist staging. Riotous and clearly avant garde, it gleefully took the subtitle of the play 'What you Will' as a justified *carte blanche*. It was repeated over and over again at the beginning of the performance, like 'Imagination' in *Pericles*: 'Twelfth Night' said Malvolio – 'Or what you will', responded the rest of the cast individually, pointing it at a member of the audience. Thus the sub-text was brought to the fore. Some, like Peter Kemp, thought it too much:

'Self-indulgence – mocked in *Twelfth Night* – is pandered to in this production' (*Independent* 17/1/87 Donmar Warehouse).

In Poland, the production proved highly controversial, audiences being divided:

'The silence hovered, crackled: at moments it broke into a ripple of applause, or a clatter of outrage as someone walked out' (Janet Watts *Observer* 19/4/87 Theatre Stodola Warsaw).

In Sicily, the opening up of the play was more gratefully appreciated:

'Cowboy hats to garden chairs, consumer magazines to plastic cups, cigarettes to champagne. In this way the story is de-idealised and removed from an a-historical, magical, evanescent and rarefied context to a more immediate setting which is clearer, more dynamic and fast moving' (*Gazetta Del Sud* 8/8/86).

And back in Poland, the distinguished Shakespeare scholar, Grzegorz Sinko, reported on the juxtaposition of direction and design:

'The language stratum of the performance as shaped by the director, and the visual stratum created by the stage designer, produced an over-all effect of a modernising transposition and not of a travesty' (*Teatr* June 1987).

The marriages and confused sexuality of the play were boldly exposed. Donnellan, talking in 1988, explained:

'You can look at a Shakespeare comedy – like *Much Ado*, *As You Like It*, or *A Midsummer Night's Dream* – as if they triumphantly uphold our modern bourgeois preconceptions of marriage. And so most of the people who write most of the introductions to most of those frightful editions of Shakespeare will say that these plays, at the end, show the Triumph of Love's order, the characters dividing neatly into heterosexual couples. But, of course, as soon as you start to examine those plays, you see that they do indeed celebrate the glory of marriage – which is the warts in it. If you look at any of the three marriages which line up on stage at the end of *Twelfth Night* – Toby and Maria, Orsino and Viola, Olivia and Sebastian – they are rather peculiar marriages, and that makes them like marriages in real life .... You reduce the play if you say that in a space of a caesura, Orsino becomes "cured" of his homosexuality and suddenly sees through to the femaleness of Viola'.

And in this production, Viola felt obliged to make Orsino feel her breast. When Viola first meets Olivia she was forced to guess which of the three veiled figures (Maria, Olivia or Feste) is 'the honourable lady of the house' – taking Shakespeare's subversiveness to the extreme. Antonio was in love with Sebastian in this production; Sir Toby shared a lads-together lechery with Feste; and Feste and Antonio paired up at the end:

'More crucially, Orsino's attraction to the "male" Viola is played as passionate love, and he constantly makes passes at "him". The disappointed tone of the Duke's functional speeches following the revelation of her true identity lends his closing description of her as "his fancy's queen" a wishful, twentieth-century resonance' (Duncan Wu *Times Literary Supplement* 23/1/87 Donmar Warehouse).

These sexual ambiguities are something which Cheek by Jowl wish to explore even further (and as it would have been on Shakespeare's stage) by having an all-male cast in *As You Like It*: 'We that are true lovers run into strange capers'.

 don't know anything about Motley Fools, but I am intrigued about playing a court jester. It's an unknown journey that we're all setting out on. All I can think is that I'm too old to woo a twenty-year-old Audrey; and Audrey is going to be a man, which will make it even more disconcerting' (Peter Needham, May 1991)

Cheek by Jowl often play with the sexual politics within the text. The all-male, fourteen-strong cast is not a unique idea in modern British theatre; but it is something which Cheek by Jowl for their tenth anniversary production of *As You Like It* approach in a distinctive way. Tom Hollander (Celia) and Adrian Lester (Rosalind), described their unusual creative journey during rehearsals in July 1991:

'I'm hoping that if I do something outrageously male then somebody will point it out to me. But my priority is to play a person. Often Adrian and I, or Richard Cant as Audrey and Sam Graham as Phebe, have done something that we thought that person would do, but we've done it physically with a male vocabulary because we are men. We then have to rethink it' (Hollander)

'It's like speaking French. You know you want to say something, so you think it in English and then speak it in French. Through Sue Lefton's movement we've been able to think about it in a detailed way as a woman' (Lester).

Joe Dixon (Jaques) recognises that the whole company has been part of the process:

'We all improvised women, and by seeing other people's mistakes those playing women could see what not to do. Declan didn't come into a rehearsal with a concept. The whole thing has evolved as a group with the director directing us through improvisation, exploration of different ideas, and going with an instinct. Declan will see the essence of what an actor is doing and pick it out, expand it, and bring it to life'.

Looking forward to *As You Like It* in March 1991, Donnellan spelled out his approach:

'By doing *As You Like It* with an all-male company, people have frightened us by asking: "What are your precise intentions?". Well, it's a play about sexuality with the extra layer of irony that Shakespeare had with women played by men. So when Orlando is wooed by Rosalind, it's actually a male actor playing Rosalind playing Ganymede, who then pretends to be Rosalind. It's actually a man playing a woman playing a man playing a woman. We have no interpretative view of it other than it would be very nice to start with that as something to be investigated. We've no idea where that will take us in rehearsal'.

At the first performance of *As You Like It*'s world tour at Farnham's Redgrave Theatre, Surrey, on July 11th 1991, men playing women became a fascinating convention quickly assimilated by the audience, and exquisitely performed by the actors.

Obviously the production will grow on tour, but even at the first performance it was clear that Cheek by Jowl had matured. No longer does a wild anarchy dominate the staging – though it still informs the freedom of imaginative association – but a more serene atmosphere, where acting is carefully carefree, pervades.

It is the strength of the casting throughout which unpicks obscurities and lays bare a text peopled by a huge range of individuals of contrasting backgrounds, desires and expectations. Amiens, singing Cunneen's extraordinary counter-tenor lines, develops a peculiar love for a prematurely melancholy Jaques, Corin, the shepherd, patiently accepts the invasion of his flock-tending livelihood by a galavanting, work-shy class of court self-indulgents. Ormerod's costume design moves from the harsh black-and-white of the ugly male machismo of a de-bagging male retinue, offset by the sumptuous blue satin of Celia's dress and the red of Rosalind's, to an overcoated, bleak Arden in winter and a joyously pale-shaded summer, softly lit by Judith Greenwood. Donnellan creates a dark drama in the light comedy, its charm and delight tinged with wistful pathos. It's never low-key, always highly-charged. And by playing the play, Cheek by Jowl's *As You Like It* is willy-nilly a collective theatrical celebration.

TURNING ON A SIXPENCE

WORKING WITH CHEEK BY JOWL

**W**hen I talk to actors I generalise because I'm using words. But they've got this wonderful canvas (like Nick has, or I might have when I'm doing some staging) where you can do something that's non-verbal, that's non-intellectual, and something which couldn't be as well-expressed if you wrote an essay about it. If you could write an essay about it, it wouldn't be a piece of theatre, would it? (Declan Donnellan)

Cheek by Jowl productions aren't directed by a split-personality artistic director, an Ormellan or a Donnerod. Ormerod is in a unique position as a designer since he is co-artistic director of the company and thus shares in choosing the plays and casting them. But in the rehearsal room, he, like anyone involved in the creative team, doesn't thwart the authority or betray the trust of the director. Ideas are freely thrown around, and Ormerod's are precise and pertinent, rarely disruptive or insensitive. 'I have put my foot in it before,' admits Ormerod, 'but I hope I've got better. Occasionally I'll come up with an idea which hopefully comes at a reasonably tactful moment.'

Ormerod would never say anything to an actor directly about his or her performance, preferring to consult Donnellan privately if necessary. Yet he does feel unfettered in making broader suggestions about the playing of a scene as a whole.

As the company has matured, the specific talents of choreographers and composers have made way for the more integral approaches of musical and movement direction from two people in particular.

PADDY CUNNEEN

Keith Bartlett was instrumental in introducing Cheek by Jowl's musical director to the company. And it wasn't the first time he'd recommended Cunneen for a theatre role: 'I was working with Paddy in a Wimbledon pub theatre. I invited Glen Walford from the Liverpool Everyman to come and see the show, and she loved the music so much that she took Paddy up there to work for a few years, where he became an Associate Director. I later introduced him to Declan.

'After *The Tempest*'s first rehearsal, we were in a pub and Paddy came up to thank me. I said: "That's all right. That's a nice shirt you've got on" – "It's yours", and he took it off right there and gave it to me in the pub. So, by the time he was doing *Peer Gynt* at the National I thought: "Right, I'm after the suit now" '.

Though Cheek by Jowl have used expert musicians in the past, Cunneen's intuition and commitment within the rehearsal space, and for the production, matches Donnellan's in direction and Ormerod's in design. For example, he avoids composing anything before rehearsals begin. 'It closes down the options of exploring in rehearsal. So I try and prepare some ideas or research (like tangos for *As You Like It*) but wait until I actually get in there with the actors before I start composing. Like the actors, I go in on day one with not much idea of how it's going to be – which is frightening. The advantage is that you tailor what you do to the company

as you go along. I think that you are much more prepared to let go of ideas if you haven't been up all night for two weeks working them out in the first place because that leads to a determination to get them in, no matter what. It gives a flexibility.

'I don't really take musical ideas from the actors. What I do is assess their level of ability and work out what they are capable of and how far they can be pushed. It's more diagnostic than interactive in that sense.'

Cunneen's not selfish about his musical ideas, often prepared for them not to be used directly in a production, if they have served their purpose in the rehearsal process. And he's adamant that while music should be rough and raw (otherwise it may as well be pre-recorded, defeating the purpose of its live theatricality) it shouldn't dominate at the expense of everything else, especially the actor. 'Like Nick doesn't go out of his way to make the design visible, I don't go out of my way to make the music stand apart from the play. It's about integrating all those things. It's from that basis that the whole is greater than the sum of its parts.'

Cunneen's music is there to be seen as well as heard: 'When you go to rock bands, the thing that really makes things work is when the bass player starts jumping, or the drummer is like Animal on *The Muppets*. It's incredibly infectious. It switches off all those musical faculties which say: "They're only using two chords here". That's what's good about theatre. When people put a lot into what they're doing, they become compulsive to watch. It becomes exciting not just because of its musical merits but because of the adrenalin that you're watching going into the making of it'.

JANE GIBSON

Gibson's movement direction in the few productions she has worked on for Cheek by Jowl is homogenous, like Cunneen's music, with the whole creative approach. She first worked with Cunneen, Ormerod and Donnellan on their National Theatre prodution of *Fuente Ovejuna*.

'There's a fantastic energy. They're very articulate, and through that communication confidence is bred. If you trust each other, you are going to gel much more than if you're constantly being careful not to upset each other. Declan's overtly appreciative of what you do, and often in front of everyone, which is an important link in the chain because then everyone has a trust in each other. Declan's got great leadership qualities, but he's also got the ability to share the whole experience with everyone.

'Nick's designs are very actor-friendly, and therefore very theatre-friendly. He doesn't stick a great big static idea in the middle of the stage whose effect wears off after a couple of minutes and can never move in the way that an actor can move. Nick is sympathetic to the human body, which is quite rare in a theatre designer. He doesn't dress actors in things that they can't move in, or can't breathe in, or can't walk in.'

Like Cunneen, Gibson has the belief that movement should be integrated totally into a production, totally absorbed into its growth, and not plastered on top separately; 'I'm not a choreographer, I'm a movement director. If that movement stands out or gets a round of applause, then I've failed in a sense because I feel that the audience shouldn't notice it. There should be one language on stage being unfolded.

'A misconception about movement is that you're only going to be excited by people standing on their heads and waggling their legs. I am interested in theatre, and the movement is there to serve the piece of theatre, and to help tell the story, to help communicate what the play is about. You're trying to open up the possibilities that the actors have in them, if they're just given the permission and the confidence to do that – to really transform physically, even if it's a minute amount. It can be quite subtle. You can do a Beckett play, for example, which is very still and where the people hardly move at all; and yet there's something fantastic in the intensity of their physical life. A lot of so-called physical theatre I can't bear, because it draws attention to itself with the form shouting at you, and you can't experience the content'.

Gibson understands that the distinction between her work with Cheek by Jowl and with other companies and directors, is inescapably made by the sense of ensemble. 'The people who come to work with Cheek by Jowl are receptive, and open, and ready to go somewhere, and then go somewhere they didn't think they were going to go in the first place. They're not brought into the company to do the thing they've always done. There's a diverse mixture of people who aren't going to put up blocks and always say "why" or "no". Declan needs a lot of "yes, let's".'

This serves the performance, which ultimately rests upon the performers.

PERFORMERS
SIMON NEEDS

When Needs went to that first Cheek by Jowl audition for *The Country Wife* at London's Drill Hall in the summer of 1981, he had no idea that this was a company who would be going places over the next ten years. However, once the production was on the road, he did suspect the company might be something special. 'We had very good reviews for *The Country Wife* – not outstanding, but very good – which was amazing with so many shows on the Edinburgh Fringe. The general feeling in the company was that we just knew something had got to happen to Declan. In fact a friend of mine who came to see it said: "Stay friends with Declan at all costs because he's going to end up at the National Theatre". People had said that about other directors before, and I suppose he could have gone down the tubes like a lot of people do; but somehow his dedication and his belief in himself – which isn't a big-headed belief; he's extremely modest – made him grow. He didn't know that the way he worked was right or wrong, but he knew that it was the only way he knew how to work.'

Needs worked with Donnellan and Ormerod in *Bent* at Exeter's Northcott Theatre in 1983. He didn't act with them again until he was cast in *Fuente Ovejuna* at the National Theatre in 1989. By then, he could see how much their knowledge of acting had matured. 'Declan doesn't have note sessions much while you're rehearsing, not until near the end. We'd all come in exhausted after a dress rehearsal or a preview and he'd give a few notes, but they were all absolutely spot on. They were the things which in the back of your mind you knew were wrong, without being able to work out what it

was. He'd immediately see what it was and be able to articulate it in such a vivid way, that you knew that that was exactly what was wrong with the entire scene. They were often not specific notes about individual lines, never "I think you should move slightly to the left because we can't see the actor behind you". They were major notes in a way, they were absolutely crucial things about a scene which he would pull out so that your imagination would be immediately sparked and you'd be able to go out there and do it completely new. I noticed in *Fuente Ovejuna* how much he hates ators doing "acting". He likes people just to be. You have to rely on the script to do the work for you and just be the character – don't present the character to the audience, don't say: "Look; I'm doing this because this is what my character does in this situation". Just be it and do it and it will come through itself.

'In the years since *The Country Wife* Declan had obviously developed and matured, and had gained a terrific amount of confidence. With *The Country Wife* I think he was constantly worried that he might not have grasped what the actor needed or wanted. He would sometimes give up: "I don't know what to do; I don't know how to direct actors". That has developed in a good way in the sense that he now doesn't give up at all. He will go at it and at it.'

AMANDA HARRIS

'When I was with Cheek by Jowl, it was quite a different set-up from now. You used to pop round to their house and chat about things over a cup of tea.' Harris joined Cheek by Jowl in 1982 to play Desdemona in *Othello*.

'I kept a notebook of the touchstones, the things to remember that help you in sticky moments. *Pericles* was very technical: "Never fade out on the end of sentences"; "Don't reproduce, recreate"; "You can only be vulnerable for moments", which is true, because you can only let people in for a certain amount of time – you've got to recover and give them time to recover too. There's a whole host of wonderful insights into actors in my notebook. I don't know where Declan got it from because it takes you years to really learn those sorts of things. "Eradicate all superfluous sounds by energising the next word with the sound'', which again is a technical thing. You'd pick up a cue like: "Yes, thank you" in response to a question rather than: "Mmm, yes, thank you". Declan would say: "Why don't you put the 'mmm' into the 'yes'?". It's just little things, but it gives the right kind of pace.

'Cheek by Jowl keep evolving. It's a bit like Madonna who keeps coming up with a new image – though not as quick as her! They always seem to be slightly ahead. You see other companies, small ones and big ones, who pick up on their ideas and copy them. It's a special quality to have, to be innovative, to be the first one to do something.

'On tour they seemed to be there constantly which was good, not only for the morale of the small group who were on the road for two years (apart from the multi-purpose stage manager, we were the crew, washing and ironing our own costumes, lugging it all in and lugging it all out of the venues – we'd trundle from one venue to another crammed in the back of this Mercedes van with three sets and Sadie Shimmin's baby!), but artistically too. We were excited to get their notes because performances would grow and change, and then grow and change more because of their constant input.

'Declan is very good at casting people who clock onto his sense of humour and ideas. He particularly likes women. A lot of directors don't. There are still those around who are terribly sexist, not giving women much kudos as actresses. You don't get that many women directors, so it's wonderful to have a man who's in tune with us.'

ANNE WHITE

From Emilia in *Othello* (joining the second tour in 1983) to coming out of Cheek by Jowl retirement to play the Queen of Naples in *The Tempest* in 1988 (and to be an assistant director on *Philoctetes*), Anne White spent over four years with Cheek by Jowl off and on as they evolved. In conversation, she performs her points as much as she says them, a true Cheek by Jowl persona.

'They call me the Dame of Cheek by Jowl. Right from *Othello* I loved it, because they were making Shakespeare come alive and immediate for the audience. The understanding was so clear. Declan

gives Shakespeare a good old shake-up and you suddenly see something new that was always there, just hidden. He also brings out the small characters so that you see the whole, with the characters you hadn't really been aware of before. And with Nick's simple designs, you become so aware of the people who populate the stage.

'Declan allows the actor to bring what they have to a part. Then he sees the better ways it could be presented, and he tells you, and you suddenly realise "of course! of course!". He's not like the director who uses actors as paint, squeezing them onto the canvas. Declan is a sculptor, with a light touch – moulding, sculpting, chiselling. I have cried in his rehearsals because he's so demanding, but in a good way which makes you stretch yourself and do things that you'd been scared of. He brings things out of you that you didn't know you had.

'He has a favourite phrase which is "Turning on a Sixpence". In other words, the quickfire of emotions rather than getting stuck into one. As people, we change so quickly: you can laugh one minute, cry the next. You instantly change, spinning on that sixpence.

'My acting has leapt bounds by working with Declan. He's taught me how things evolve and grow. Sometimes it can be so hard because it seems he's getting at you and you think "I can't, I can't". He shows you that you can.'

DUNCAN BELL

Bell appeared in *Vanity Fair*, *Pericles* and *Andromache* (and the beginning of the *Midsummer Night's Dream* tour) early on in his career. While performing on London's Fringe, Bell saw Cheek by Jowl's *Othello* at Hampstead's New End Theatre in January 1983, and promptly wrote Donnellan a letter saying how much he would like to work with him. Come May, Donnellan called Bell to audition for *Vanity Fair*, opening at that August's Edinburgh Festival. Most other members of the cast had worked with Donnellan before – Simon Dormandy and Bell were the new boys.

From *Vanity Fair* the tour and output of work 'escalated immensely – it was quite amazing. It was a pragmatic experience. You'd set yourself an impossible task and see how much you could achieve. *Andromache* was introduced to the repertoire to contrast with *Pericles* and *Vanity Fair* – it was still, intense, concentrated and demanded listening. It wasn't up-front like the others.

'Declan always grasps the innocence of the story-telling, the active narrative, the comic urge. His is instant, recognisable communication. He doesn't insist on analysing the text. It's very much an on-your-feet experience. There's a directness of communication in the urgency with which you compel attention, both on an individual and group level of commitment. That's something instantly recognisable about Declan's style: a group of people gather together to tell a story, which should be like an experience which has just happened.'

SASKIA REEVES

Saskia Reeves' first 'proper job', she considers, was with Cheek by Jowl. She'd been working with Simon Dormandy for the Covent Garden Community Theatre Company, who mentioned to her that he was going to audition for Declan Donnellan's Cheek by Jowl production of *Vanity Fair*: ' "Who's Declan Donnellan? What's Cheek by Jowl?", I asked. And after Simon told me about them, I thought how I'd love to audition. Declan actually came to see one of our shows at the Oval House. The show got cancelled and we all went to the pub. Simon was talking to Declan, and I just stared at this man. I managed to get my agent to get me an audition, and I think Declan was very interested, but I had to wait a year and a half before he 'phoned me up and asked me to come along and audition for *The Dream*.

'Up till then I'd been doing bits and pieces and I hated it, and I remember thinking "if this is what acting's about, I don't want to do it". I started rehearsing with Cheek by Jowl at the beginning of 1985 and remember standing in this church hall doing the first scene of *A Midsummer Night's Dream* with all these actors and Declan turning what on paper wasn't all that interesting into an extraordinary event, and I couldn't believe it. I also fell in love with one of the actors in the first few weeks of rehearsal. So, not only was I head-over-heels in love, but I was also doing the best work that I'd ever

done before with this amazing man and these wonderful people and I just spent four weeks laughing. I thought: "So this is what it's like to be an actress".

'Declan knows what he's thinking in terms of pictures and laughs, shapes and stories. If your imagination is as alive as his, then it can be irresistible working with someone like that. I remember that he used to twiddle things all the time. He always seemed to be playing with a coathanger wandering around the room and twisting it'.

Reeves thinks that Donnellan's energy comes from an over-active imagination. She recalls the three types of actors that Stanislavsky outlined, with their three types of imagination: 'There's one sort of imagination that is flying here, there and everywhere. It's people who have a very strong fantasy life. Declan is one of those people and a lot of his actors are like that. I'm more of the second type, who has a strong imagination but needs it to be drawn out. If you suggest something to us we go "brilliant", but if we're asked to invent all on our own we'd walk around pulling out our hair. It's not a lazy imagination; it just needs help. And then there's the third type, which doesn't get stimulated at all'.

Touring with *A Midsummer Night's Dream*, and then *The Man of Mode* as well must have been pretty arduous, but Reeves' enthusiasm was never to be dampened: 'We used to have to iron our own costumes because you'd get them out of the trunk all wrinkled. So it would be: "I'm on the iron first" – "No, no you can't, I've got to". I also remember getting down on my hands and knees and cleaning the white floor of the set'.

KEITH BARTLETT

Bartlett performed with Cheek by Jowl from *Twelfth Night* to *The Tempest* and *Philoctetes* (he'd taken a break during *A Family Affair*). Bartlett first worked with Donnellan and Ormerod at Exeter's Northcott Theatre, in *Bent*. Donnellan and Ormerod were surprised when, after having been impressed by their *Midsummer Night's Dream*, Bartlett asked them if he could audition for *Twelfth Night*. Bartlett isn't an older actor by any means, but nor was he

green, fresh out of drama school, and in his early twenties. Cheek by Jowl tended to favour very young performers, not just because they were affordable and willing to tour (without mortgages or school uniforms to worry about) but also because they have an eagerness which some older actors, perhaps, might not have, less willing to throw themselves into a Cheek by Jowl production and make themselves look silly (though lately, it hasn't stopped people like Daniel Thorndike adoring the company).

'When I made enquiries about the casting of *Twelfth Night*,' explains Bartlett, 'Declan said: "Oh you don't want to go and sit in a minibus driving round the country". And I said: "Yeah!", and still felt it four months later after 16,000 miles.'

Bartlett appreciates that the initial audition was Donnellan and Ormerod's way of establishing whether the actor was right for them and they were right for the actor. 'They put you through quite a process in audition. Declan throws some ridiculous things at you. Some people think he must be mad. He loves actors who are able to drop their trousers in front of an audience – not literally (often).'

TIMOTHY WALKER

From Orsino in *Twelfth Night* to Hamlet, Walker, the mildest of men, has played a huge range of characters with varying degrees of dementia. Walker himself has an astute mind, and it's from his unpublished article, *Potent Art*, that the following is extracted: 'I did my audition speech – Troilus – as I'd done so many times before, when suddenly he said: "What perfume was she wearing last night?" – "Who?" – "Cressida". Then he made me do a ghastly improvisation, repeat the first four lines over and over again, each time changing what I was doing: sometimes to attack, sometimes to seduce, sometimes to astonish, sometimes to frighten; and finally had me rolling on the floor screaming – all at the unfortunate Cressida, who was a chair. Waiting on the platform for my train home after this, my first encounter with Declan Donnellan, I felt strangely exhilarated. The next few years were to prove the most enriching, challenging, infuriating and formative period of theatrical experience I have had.

'Opening *The Tempest* on a real island in the Mediterranean overlooking the sea was a sensual delight. But more dangerous was *Twelfth Night* in Warsaw, when Feste's entrance in drag precipitated uproar which ended with two people storming out while the rest of the audience retaliated with a burst of defiant applause and roared their approval. More moving still was our reception in Bulgaria. On this first visit of a theatre company from a capitalist country for some years we were met with roses and we played to capacity with all aisles crammed; despite the deafening buzz of over a thousand simultaneous translation relays, the audience leapt to their feet in appreciation. In Kuala Lumpur, not so long ago part of the British Empire, Ariel's reply to Prospero's promise of freedom – "That's my noble master" – was met with laughter.

'Having travelled the world, communicating with people in all sorts of ways in all sorts of places – gaining, as Jaques says, "my experience" – I realise the greatest joy of it all has been the rediscovery of why I wanted to be an actor. I found an environment in which I could grow'.

In conversation, Walker expands upon his own development as an actor, explaining the means of discovery. 'One of the reasons that Cheek by Jowl's theatre works and penetrates is because it has the power of its convictions. There is a vision behind the work, which is not about the solution but the search and the exploration. It genuinely questions everything. It's committed to the question, and along the way it may find some temporary solutions. It's not afraid of mystery or not knowing. You give yourself up to something you don't know the answer to.'

DUNCAN DUFF

Duncan Duff nearly joined Cheek by Jowl during the foreign tour of *Twelfth Night* when he was auditioned, while still at RADA, on the strength of his acting combined with his clarinet- and saxophone-playing ability: 'When I auditioned for *Twelfth Night*, I had to take my passport to the audition. Nick Ormerod really freaked me out because he was so quiet. I thought Declan Donnellan quite liked me but that Nick thought I was crap'.

Impressed, but feeling the part in *Twelfth Night* could more usefully go to someone else, Donnellan and Ormerod kept Duff in mind, and he was subsequently cast in his first job, with the Equity Card that went with it, in *Macbeth* (to play the trumpet as the army approached, and to play the cream-faced loon, amongst other parts). He has since been in *Philoctetes* (where he appeared naked as the god Hercules) and *The Tempest* (a nonchalant butler, Caliban) *Sara*, and *Hamlet* (a full-blooded Horatio, rather than just Hamlet's side-kick).

'There is a ritual which is always the same in essence about the first day of a Cheek by Jowl rehearsal period. It's to get everybody loosened up, to introduce everybody gently to each other. That's done by playing silly games. Nick has one where he numbers the walls 1, 2, 3 and 4 – and the ceiling and floor 5 and 6. Nick calls out the numbers and we all touch the appropriate wall, ceiling or floor. It gets everyone running around and giggling. Paddy's got loads of rhythmic games – lots of clapping.

'Then into the first day, something relevant to the production is thrown in. On the first day of the *Macbeth* rehearsals we did some Scottish Country Dancing. With *The Tempest* we did lots of rhythm work with Paddy, and a can-can. Ultimately none of it need be really relevant. The desired effect is to get that first day over with and get into the rehearsals painlessly. With *Hamlet* we did general work for the first few days and so we didn't come to read the play until everyone really knew each other and weren't cripplingly self-conscious. I always enjoy it and it's different with each play as you're interacting with different people, so the whole dynamic of the company is different.

'Declan will never do things gratuitously. He may use scores of different techniques to rehearse. There's always a purpose and the actors can see that. You can take what you do seriously, but you find a joy and a freedom in it. In rehearsals, it's often one step forward and two steps back. Sometimes the imagination dries up and you run into problems. Or Declan might be tired. You can't play every day.'

SALLY DEXTER

The effervescent Sally Dexter had been at the National Theatre for three years when *Fuente Ovejuna* came into production. She vaguely knew Donnellan, Ormerod and Cunneen because, as she says, she would 'camp about the canteen' (Jane Gibson was more familiar to her since she had worked extensively at the National and had taught Dexter at LAMDA). Dexter's boyfriend was in *Fuente*, and perhaps Dexter felt that she knew more about them through him. On leaving the National for a season at Regent's Park Open Air Theatre, Dexter was aware of rumours about Cheek by Jowl mounting 'a musical' – and she loves singing. So, when she got the call to audition, she was thrilled, and for Dexter, emotions don't come in half-measure: 'I went round to their wonderful house in Primrose Hill and they told me about the story of Lady Betty. That story, and what I read from the script, excited me hugely. My heart beat and I knew it was going to be something special'.

As *Lady Betty* came to an end, Dexter was so fearful of the anticlimax that was bound to follow, that at one point she vowed never to act again, since she knew nothing would ever be so good.

Dexter, just as Amanda Harris had done on her first professional job with Cheek by Jowl in the early eighties, kept a notebook of the things that were both pertinent to *Lady Betty*, and the things she knew she would treasure throughout her career (with which, happily, she did decide to continue): 'I didn't use to take notes at all, but Declan was so specific in directing his notes that you had to write them down. What Declan's basically concerned with about acting is not to act at all, but to believe, to commit yourself 100% to yourself, to who you're talking to, to the whole situation. Declan was always going on about "Top Energy" and "Bottom Energy": the top energy is when you're HERE I AM LOOK AT ME!; the bottom energy is rooted. It gives a sort of structure which means that you're in control and then you can go much further. The more control I was in, the more out of control the character could be. "You should really try to cross the 'ish' out of everything", is another note I took from Declan. 'He was always saying that the only quality he had as a director was the ability to tell when somebody was lying, when someone wasn't in the moment believing. There was one specific thing which kept changing in *Lady Betty*: the Dawn scene. I don't think I ever got it right because I got muddled up with the new words. But he'd say: "Trust in the words, because a word is only an expression of what's going on inside. Trust yourself to believe in it". And another thing: "Find the script surprising" – which I usually did when it was rewritten about 3,000 times.

'Declan takes care of everyone. He didn't buy boxes of chocolates for them all the time or anything like that. It was a proper, relevant, sincere care over what was going on with everybody on the stage. He'd always be brutally honest, not like some directors who make a deliberate decision to humiliate you, but for the good of the play. He'd never attack you personally. He'd just be getting at your work. And he'd make that distinction: "Let's have less Sally and more Betty". We never really discussed things like character because it was all there in the play. I was glad about that because it's like being at school when directors say: "Now, what do you think your character had for breakfast this morning?". And you say: "Erm . . . Cornflakes?". And the director says: "Good, yes, good". And you think: "Oh, I've got it right". And then you're asked another question and you have to think of a right answer. Declan always says that you can never get it right. It's not a question of getting it right – there are a million ways of getting it right.

'One of the most frustrating things as an actress is that you can never become somebody else. If you ever really managed it you'd pop, become mad or completely doolally. But you do always strive towards it. Lady Betty was perfect for that because she had everything. She could take all I had, and more.

'In other companies the designer usually comes along on day one with little pictures and shows you what you're going to wear and what the set's going to be before you've even started. Then you try and get on with your few weeks of rehearsal with your director, and all of a sudden you get sent off for a costume fitting. Then another day the music person will come in and plop a bit of music like a top hat on it. Who knows if it fits? And somebody might come in and do a bit of dancing one day, and then you'll never see them again. With *Lady Betty* we had

Declan, Nick, Paddy and Jane, and all the actors all there all the time. Nothing's a secret. When there's a problem, everybody turns to each other and says: "Oh, I don't know what to do – let's try this". None of the "we'll let you know when we've decided". It's a vital, living decision. It's come to grips with by everybody. It's not a form of democracy where we all sit around having big discussions about the colour of the carpet. It's arrived at organically. That makes all the difference, because you then don't have those awful situations where you've been pretending to run up the stairs that you saw on the model of the set at the beginning of the rehearsals, only to find that the costume department has put you in roller-skates. You work with the music, movement and design as it happens, and they watch and they see what's coming out of what you're doing and it develops'.

PETER NEEDHAM

Thirty-five years on from his RADA training, Needham joined Cheek by Jowl (he's playing Touchstone in *As You Like It* after Polonius in *Hamlet* and Waitwell in *Sara* before that). His career has never been in the doldrums, but, on his own admission, he 'became a bit of a recluse' working at the National Theatre from 1974 to 1987. He does prefer to work in ensembles for long periods of time (he has also spent two seasons at Stratford Ontario, and four years with the Belgrade Theatre, Coventry). He'd never seen a Cheek by Jowl production when he came to meet Donnellan and Ormerod for *Sara* (by way of invitation from Daniel Thorndike, who was playing Sir William Sampson, and had had Needham as a side-kick at least once before at the National). Needham knew that Cheek by Jowl were mounting *Hamlet* in six months time too, and he boldly asked at the *Sara* meeting if he could play Polonius.

Needham's aware that it's unusual for an older actor to remain with Cheek by Jowl for more than a couple of productions. But, unjaded by his experience, he has warmed to their approach. 'In my career I've become hard-skinned about what to expect from rehearsals, always ready for anything. Though I must say that Declan's rehearsals, up to a point, took me by surprise. It was a very pleasant surprise because they were so unstuffy, so unorthodox, and so unconventional that there was a freedom. The first day was relaxing too. Even after thirty-five years, each first day of rehearsal is still like the first day of term. Nick and Declan put you at your ease.'

Perhaps it's being unnecessarily ageist (after all, Needham is only in his middle years) to expect him to have been bored by the games that Cheek by Jowl play on that first day: 'Daniel and I, as the older members, were rushing about and playing silly games too. Actors are always very childlike, willing to enter into the spirit. It's very refreshing, especially after having endured so many readthroughs sat around a table, where everyone starts to give instant performances, impressing each other with their reading ability'. Everyone joins in those first days – not just the actors, Donnellan, Ormerod, Cunneen and the production crew, but the office staff too: Matthews and her administrative team.

Needham admires Donnellan as a director, which is a respect founded upon his experience. 'Directors usually come with a very strong idea of how they are going to do the play and will often force a production into their idea, into their concept, and then make the actors go that way. Declan does not do that. He creates an environment where all sorts of things can and mostly do happen, and then we go in that direction collectively. What is then hard for the individual actor is to get the director to take his own needs on board. Yet one of Declan's great strengths is that he can respond to the individual actor. What Peter Needham wants is what Peter Needham wants; my needs are my needs; somehow Declan is intuitive enough to realise those needs in each of his individual actors.'

Cheek by Jowl is committed to the performance of the production of their chosen play. It is the actors who have the last responsibility for that. All the music, movement, direction, design, technical and administrative input is there to enable the performer:

'The dream of a true ensemble will probably never be realised as it is financially impossible to retain a large enough group of actors permanently. But I see my job as that of an enabler. I must maximise our resources and think

innovatively of ways to increase them. We have tried to make the company the star of the show' (Barbara Matthews, from *Exhibit A: A Real Live Arts Manager*).

BEYOND

CHEEK

BY

JOWL

 heek by Jowl were one of the finds of
the decade. Indeed along with Théâtre de Compli-
cité (and one might add Tara Arts and Temba)
Cheek by Jowl had turned the empty space into a
playground for the imagination producing silky
shows [...] Theatre is about telling stories and
these companies have succeeded by telling old
ones under new lights (Khalid Omar Jared *What's
On* 6/6/90)

There is much dynamic theatre beyond the work
of Cheek by Jowl. There are other companies who
could lay claim to a substantial period of creative
and influential development. They have all pursued
various strands of theatre work which all hold a
significant place in recent cultural history. From
Lloyd Webber to the Liverpool Everyman; the
Glasgow Citizens to the Theatre Royal, Stratford
East; the Royal Court, Soho Theatre Company,
Paines Plough and the Bush; Talawa, Temba, Tram-
way and Tron, Traverse, Trestle, Tara Arts and
Théâtre de Complicité; the Manchester Royal
Exchange and the RSC; the National Theatre,
Jonathan Miller's Old Vic, and the Dunlop/Bog-
danov/Thacker Young Vic; The Kosh and Kick, ATC
and Red Shift, Shared Experience and Hull Truck,
Theatr Clwyd and Volcano; the London Actors
Theatre Company, Polka, and TIE; the ballet companies, the opera companies, the circus companies;
the small-, middle- and large-scale touring companies; The Place, the Almeida and Battersea Arts
Centre; the Orange Tree and the Gate; the Fringe,
the Alternative, and idiosyncratic theatres; the
regional theatres, the commercial sector, the shoe-
string operations; the festivals and foreign companies; radio, television and film; and a multitude of

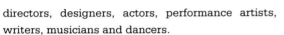

directors, designers, actors, performance artists, writers, musicians and dancers.

Yet while much of this work (and of course there are others) has collectively impressed, more has disappointed and few have sustained artistic development over a period of ten years, moving from one stage to the next. It wouldn't be right to single out one company at the expense of all the others, since it's rare for exactly the same game to be played by any two company teams under the collective umbrella of Theatre. It would be wrong to suggest that one company alone kept the homefires burning. But you can gain a view of what was best about the whole by concentrating on the very few important parts. In the diminishing pool of resourceful theatre since 1979, Cheek by Jowl – and the work in which Donnellan and Ormerod have been involved outside their company – has been a fish that's got bigger: sometimes swimming with the eddies, sometimes against; but most often creating the ripples itself.

On the one hand, their work has influenced countless practitioners, just as they have been receptive to the work of others. On the other, they have made incursions into the playhouses of opera, onto the stages of regional theatres, even (most recently) into the medium of film. And they've invaded the National Theatre, exemplary theatre artists of their age. They're not alone – but nor are they little fish in the big theatrical pool.

Donnellan and Ormerod worked in opera in the mid-eighties, bringing to that too often escapist, exclusive and expensive world their special brand of simplicity. One of their productions, Brecht and Weill's *The Rise and Fall of Mahagonny* for the Wex-

ford Festival in 1985 excited the *Guardian*'s reviewer Tom Sutcliffe:

'It was sober, straightforward and out to the audience. I was incredibly impressed'.

Sutcliffe's review noted the distress which the anti-capitalist opera caused a bourgeois Wexford audience, some of whom left, either because of the subject or because of its realisation (a few soft-porn projections, some punkish gals in scant attire). He noted that it was 'not dressed up as fantasy' but 'the theatre of demonstration, of the street and music-hall'. And it was characteristically cheap – not in effect, but to produce, Ormerod's ingenuity providing some highly adaptable tables and chairs (*Guardian* 2/11/85).

Ormerod and Donnellan have also designed and directed *Don Giovanni* for Scottish Opera-Go-Round and *A Masked Ball* for Opera 80. Ormerod designed Nicholas Hytner's production of *The Magic Flute* for the Royal Academy of Music, and *The Barber of Seville* for a Welsh National Opera tour. After training at the Wimbledon School of Art (once he'd rejected the Bar) he spent a season at the Edinburgh Lyceum and later designed *The History of Mr Polly* at York Theatre Royal and *Becoming* at the Nottingham Playhouse. With Donnellan directing, he designed *Bent* at Exeter's Northcott in 1983.

Simon Needs and Keith Bartlett performed in that early freelance production. They both agree that Exeter is not the first place that would spring to mind to mount Martin Sherman's exploration of the treatment of homosexuals in Nazi Germany. Donnellan and Ormerod came to it without their Cheek by Jowl brief, just as hired provincial rep artists. But they brought to it their theatrical integrity, as

Needs recalls:

'Declan tried to get the truth out of the play. The first two or three scenes are very domestic and he directed it like that. The set was slightly more complicated than I'd ever seen Nick do, in that the first few scenes had a lot of different settings: a flat; a railway carriage; a drag club. There was also a flat wooden floor from out of which a whole park bench flipped up. Then in the second half, set in the concentration camp, the stage was stripped bare to the back wall, with nothing on stage but barbed wire. It was very powerful.

'Exeter's a very conservative area (I'd done two plays there before) and I have to say that it wasn't that well attended. I think we did about 30–40% box office. But the people who did come were completely gobsmacked. It was so moving. As you came front of house after the performance, people would be crying'.

In this, his first job with Donnellan and Ormerod, Keith Bartlett was

'bowled over by the amount of detail and care and understanding of the script, and the clarity of the story that they would always insist on',

demands in their work that Donnellan and Ormerod continued to pursue throughout the eighties with Cheek by Jowl and beyond.

A popular production of *Romeo and Juliet* at the Regent's Park Open Air Theatre in 1986 – where Lady Capulet was as memorable a figure as her husband or her son, Donnellan continuing to appreciate the depth of characterisation well into the darker recesses of the play – was followed by productions of *Macbeth* and then *Philoctetes* in the late eighties with the Finnish National Theatre. (These two productions preceded Cheek by Jowl's.) The Cheek by Jowl performers who were touring their *Twelfth Night* in Finland at the time of the Finnish *Macbeth*, recall the sensational production:

'I remember sitting there and I just got shivers up my spine. It was wonderful, even though it was in Finnish!' (Anne White).

It was also in Finland that Donnellan and Ormerod came across *A Family Affair*.

Talking to Ralph Berry in 1988, Donnellan recounted his and Ormerod's formative experiences with actors across the world:

'We have worked on scenes in Spanish from *Romeo and Juliet* with actors from the Uruguayan National Theatre, in a real orange grove, with a real balcony. In Sri Lanka we worked on the same play with a Sinhalese Romeo and a Tamil Juliet. In Turkey we had a long session working out a production of *Hamlet* set in the decaying Ottoman Empire [. . .] In Delhi we discovered the relevance of the caste system to Malvolio's position in a rich household [. . .] In Kathmandu we did a workshop on the *deus ex machina* in *Pericles*, until we realised that the king's son was among the audience and were solemnly informed that, being a god himself, divine intervention had little shock value [. . .] And with our old friends of the Finnish National Theatre, we scraped our way through *Macbeth* in a non-Indo-European language with a saintly interpreter.

'Certain principles have become abundantly clear to us and perhaps the chief of them is this. In the beginning was not the word. In the beginning was the imagination, which longs to communicate with others. Words are one means of doing this. But no word is ever properly understood unless it has been spontaneously created by the imagination. It is possible to have a good grasp of a scene in a totally alien language if the actors' imaginations are genuinely working. There are small technical spin-offs from this: bad diction is normally caused not by a shaky palate but by a sloppy imagination.

'The actor can get an audience to believe anything, but only if the actor is prepared to believe it himself. This is the basis of all our work and we have learnt it among strangers' (*On Directing Shakespeare*).

It is this experience with actors of many backgrounds which Donnellan and Ormerod most value. And it's one they have further enhanced with the opportunities coming from working with larger acting companies. One has been at Britain's National Theatre. It is here that they have found their second home.

THE NATIONAL THEATRE

'The best ensemble playing I've seen at the NT for a long time' (Lyn Gardner *City Limits*

19/1/89 *Fuente Ovejuna*)

'This is one of the best ensemble productions I have seen in Britain' (Michael Billington *Guardian* 2/3/90 *Peer Gynt*)

The National Theatre (now with the unnecessary prefix of 'Royal') has an Artistic Director who's keen to run a catholic church, hosting a number of national theatre companies within three theatres, rather than one company with one identity within the same building. Richard Eyre has been given praise for taking on the best of the nation's theatre – praise has also been witheld by those who, perhaps churlishly, feel that he's only come round to accepting what his predecessor ignored. He's taken on a number of Fringe graduates (proving themselves on the Fringe of mainstream theatre, not a graduation that makes them qualified and grown-up enough to move into the mainstream) just at the right time in their blossoming careers – careers which were never careerist, never with the hope of playing those stages of the National as their impetus. These graduates are not prepared to be compromised, which is why their theatre suceeds wherever it is staged, their art not forestalled or dissipated.

That's rare, because there is a danger that when these people join the national institutions their creativity is curtailed. Moreover, the innovative Fringe could be castrated, thus ceasing to provoke the development of theatre at large. Shrewdly, most of those practitioners have continued to run their own companies. So although they've changed sides, as it were, they're still the opposition.

Perhaps Fringe (a misleading negative differential, wrongly assuming that the centre of the theatre, to which it is on the fringes by comparison, is better) has become fashionable and National Theatre-worthy. It no longer behaves badly as it did in the sixties and seventies, and it's rarely rude or alternative (you have to look at the disparate movements in performance – mime, dance, devised work and all its permutations of mutated text-based work – for a real alternative). Cheek by Jowl does go some way towards the hot-headedness and intellectual vulgarity of that inheritance. They do enjoy experiment, from coy tinkering to hard-hitting transformation. They do give a two-fingered

gesture to more orthodox ideals with their perky rehearsal-room antics. It's not a fully-blown cultural vandalism like a Charles Marowitz mêlée of Shakespeare; but it is an avant-garde joviality.

There is a realisation now in the nineties, that Cheek by Jowl's well-earned audience is always going to expect the unexpected (and thus *Hamlet*, to many, was disappointing and grey). It's part of a neo-classical bandwagon that built up a full head of steam in the eighties along with the opera of the Tim Alberys, and David Freemans with his Opera Factories. Donnellan and Ormerod have moved from the small to the big spaces successfully (either with *Romeo & Juliet* at Regent's Park's Open Air Theatre, or with *Peer Gynt* in the National's Olivier). Thus their work has a very literal potential for expansion.

Richard Eyre makes no excuses for having taken on the Ormerods and Donnellans out of 'self-interest':

'Your sole purpose and motivation in running a theatre is presenting something that's alive. Clearly a live theatre, rather than a mausoleum, implies one that has a sense of invention, of the medium being re-invented. I don't understand theatre that invokes the past, what it's doing in a medium that takes place in the present. So, I looked around at a generation – not my own – of directors whose work I found the most alive. Declan and Nick were two of those people. That's where the self-interest comes in. How do I re-animate the National Theatre? Well, I get these bright fellas to come and work here. It is opportunism'.

Eyre has also taken on Donnellan as an Associate Director, along with Nicholas Hytner, Howard Davies and Deborah Warner (the other associates being primarily writers, actors and designers):

'I found that we got on very well together and I wanted Declan to be identified over a longer period with the continuity of work at the National. It's sort of family, I guess. You sort of know who you want to go to bed with. When I invited him to come and do *Fuente Ovejuna*, I didn't know that I would invite him to become an Associate Director. But that went well and I had a great deal of rapport with Declan and Nick, and they seemed to be immensely supportive of what

I was doing. Declan seemed like a colleague, a comrade, and it seemed logical to ask him to join the cabinet'.

That support which Donnellan and Ormerod can give, coupled with admiration for their work, prompted Sam Wanamaker, the American actor turned Bardophile entrepreneur, to invite them to join the Artistic Directorate of his new Shakespeare Globe Theatre. On the south bank of the Thames in Bermondsey, Wanamaker has at last realised his (and many others') dream of building a theatre which recreates the environment and the proportions of the stage upon which it's likely that most of Shakespeare's plays were originally performed. It's on a site adjacent to the old Bear Gardens (where The Shakespeare Globe Trust have their offices), a monstrous office block which now covers the fleetingly excavated Rose Theatre, and the original Globe site under a road bridge.

The project has aroused much controversy over the years, both from the local community and councillors who were upset that a prime site should be used for a cultural centre rather than much-needed new housing, and from theatrical cynics, doubting that the building would be much more than a tourist attraction for those on the Shakespeare Trail, presenting doublet-and-hose cod-piece performances in an effort of historical authenticity.

Whatever the feelings and arguments that have dogged the project, Wanamaker has been aware of them all, and on the artistic question at least he is proving himself to be progressive rather than regressive.

He has gathered together a variegated collection of theatre professionals who act as an artistic directorate, thirty people who include Judi Dench, Derek Jacobi, Steven Berkoff, Jane Lapotaire, Nicholas Hytner, Deborah Warner, Declan Donnellan and the only designer amongst the team, Nick Ormerod.

Wanamaker, greatly encouraged so far by the policy contribution of his committed team who display great integrity about the future of the theatre, sees Donnellan and Ormerod as kindred spirits:

'We're not going to do museum theatre. That's not the basic objective of our experimental facility to explore the plays of Shakespeare and his period. Declan's been doing just that sort of exploration with his work for Cheek by Jowl and at the National, without the gimmicky, hefty tricks that the original Globe would never have seen and wouldn't be appropriate for the new Globe. He and Nick recognise the humanity of the plays. The plays aren't made relevant; they are relevant. The Globe represents a challenge for all the artistic elements involved since no-one has really had the experience of playing to an audience standing on three sides with stacks of crowded galleries. There won't be any mysterious smoke, clever recorded sound effects, lighting tricks and all those boring clichés.

'Nick and Declan's work has been terribly impressive. There's a clear affinity between a Globe staging and what they do, using a platform and a minimal set. They display the content of the plays through language and performance with a rare quality of freshness and excitement.

'Nick's sets don't violate the space but enhance the stories and their themes. He's much more imaginative than that, adding useful not gratuitous elements. They really are a splendid duo to have involved'.

It wasn't just their production of a Shakespeare (*The Tempest* at the Donmar) which convinced Wanamaker of Ormerod and Donnellan's suitability for his project. It was the warmth of their *Fuente Ovejuna* too.

Fuente Ovejuna was a theatrical celebration, despite being a dark play encompassing the humanity of a peasant community who turn on the aristocratic overlords investigating the consequences of the rape of Laurencia. It was played in traverse in the Cottesloe, with a huge backcloth of a colourful and earthy Spanish country landscape suddenly unfurling from the ceiling at one end, and the thrones of Ferdinand and Isabella in their aristocratic black costumes with white ruffs at the other. The contrasting colours, the movement and the music were inseparable from the drama:

'The reaping, grinding movements of the peasants' daily work become magnified into the terrible repetitive actions of slaughter when the commander is attacked; the traditional folk dances are transformed into symbols of defiance;

the appalling torture of the entire town is all the more distressing because Donnellan cleverly leaves it up to the audience's imagination to supply the physical details' (Lyn Gardner *City Limits* 19/1/89).

Neil Kinnock, on one of his many visits to the theatre, 'very much enjoyed their excellent production' and in its opening week there seemed to be a three-line whip on the Shadow Cabinet, most of them attending a performance.

Simon Needs, once again part of a Donnellan and Ormerod rehearsal after an absence of six years, believes that:

'*Fuente Ovejuna* was never going to become another National Theatre production, in the sense of being institutionalised. I think that we felt a lot of the National's productions were the same at the time. Declan rang me before rehearsals started and joked: "I don't even know my way backstage, what am I going to do?". But I don't think that he was afraid that his style would become subsumed under a relatively huge budget. They both just had what they'd had with Cheek by Jowl, only with more actors and technical support. I only had a small part in it — but everybody had small parts, and we were all excited by it on the very first day of rehearsals when we immediately launched into Flamenco dancing.'

Rachel Joyce playing Laurencia, the apparent focus of the story since it is her rape which symbolises the rape of the community, recognised that each member of that community on stage was focussed:

'What Declan brought to that was his interest in how individuals work within a large community. You could watch everybody *en masse* because there was something fascinating about each individual'.

She thinks that this community may have been established on the very first day of rehearsal:

'Jane Gibson began with an old peasant dance where you started off on your right foot and walked amongst each other in a pattern. It immediately established contact with everyone — not only physically, because by constantly passing people you became accustomed to faces and you registered them. You were all taking part in something together, and meeting people rather than being isolated'.

Gibson expands on that process:

'It was all built up layer by layer. A physical language was discovered then laid down, built up from. The nobles and the peasants had different bodies. We worked on what it was like for someone to labour from morning to night, on that landscape and in that light. They would then take an imaginary tool, an implement, and find the rhythm of that by using it for a good half hour, and then imagine what it was like doing it for one half hour after another. And then working on a land which didn't belong to you, so that everything you did was for the benefit of somebody else. Then the nobles would pass through and everything they could see, they owned. So we worked on what it was like for someone never to have to lift a finger.

'We did a lot of Spanish dance, and Renaissance court dance, and married the two together. And the rhythms were explored with Paddy. And all mixed together in Nick and Declan's staging. We were all equally giving together'.

Donnellan and Ormerod's *Fuente Ovejuna* was a phenomenal success — it won Donnellan the Olivier Award for Outstanding Achievement, in memory of Kenneth Tynan, in 1990, and is to be remounted in 1992 and taken to Seville. When Donnellan suggested it to Eyre along with a number of other plays he would like to stage, Eyre was keen that he should do it with the bigger resources of the National rather than with Cheek by Jowl. Eyre already knew the play:

'I first heard about *Fuente* when I was doing Dusty Hughes' *Futurists*, about the lead up to the Russian Revolution. I read about performances of *Fuente Ovejuna* on the streets of Leningrad so I was rather attracted to this play which seemed to me a piece of early, revolutionary street theatre; and because it was about a community. Adrian Mitchell sent me a translation he'd done which he'd updated to central America, which just irritated me. So, he went back and translated the original play. Simultaneously, Declan suggested that he'd like to direct the play.

'I do think that *Fuente Ovejuna* was one of the most satisfying, one of the most thoroughly truthful productions of a classical play that I've ever seen. It was entirely true to itself, to its period, to its inherent meanings, while at the same time being in the present tense. It was extremely accomplished'.

William Gaskill, rehearsing at the National at the time, wrote in the *Guardian* that:

'Declan Donnellan triumphantly combines black and white actors in *Fuente Ovejuna*, and creates a world of aristocrats and peasants that feels wholly Spanish' (19/8/89).

Donnellan and Ormerod brought their Cheek by Jowl brand of fully-integrated casting to the National, an un-self-conscious casting based on talent, not colour or race. A *New York Times* article on the lack of ambition in integrated casting in British theatre quoted Donnellan's position:

' ''Fully integrated casting means you actually ask actors to do what they are rarely asked to do – act – instead of being who they are [...] I started integrated casting because there were the most wonderful black actors who were frustrated because they were not getting parts in the classical repertory. That is the only reason. I'm not doing black people a favour. All of the black actors we use would have got parts out of natural competition, standing up against white actors.

' ''The first stage in dealing with the problem we have is coming to the acceptance that we are all racists [...] We have to accept that we are completely conditioned by our society. It's hard for people to see black actors in certain roles because they don't see them often enough. You need imagination to see that a person playing a mugger or murderer for the fifteenth time on television could also play the king of England'' ' (8/9/90).

In a quasi-manifesto on theatre which Donnellan had written for *Time Out* in 1989, *Staging Revolution*, he drew special attention to this aspect of casting for his ideal theatre of the future:

'Theatre Which Takes Integrated Casting For Granted. The arguments for this are too obvious to be mentioned. *Likelihood*: Extremely likely, in fact this is the only area where I feel quite sure

that the theatre of 2000 will be better than that of 1990. Now some all-white companies seem odd. All leaps of the imagination seem smaller looking backwards, and already an audience is less likely to comment on, say, mixed race families on stage than was the case some years ago. There is still a struggle, but the bitterest struggle is inside ourselves' (18/10/90).

Eyre appreciates the credibility that Donnellan has brought to the National's casting policy, though he insists it's because Donnellan has enjoyed a freer hand by directing classic plays:

'Declan's quite evangelical about it and it seems to be triumphantly vindicated. It is the policy of the theatre as a whole, but it doesn't apply to every play. It's not about whether non-white actors are good or not; it all comes down to aesthetics. In a lot of circumstances I would entirely endorse that casting policy. In others, I couldn't. In *Racing Demon* you can't cast a black actor in Michael Bryant's part, the Reverend Harry Henderson, because it is just a lie. There is no black vicar in their fifties in the Church of England today; so it's a lie to put that on stage. That's an area where you would be having a discussion about multi-racial casting and whether it is true to the play you are doing, or whether it's nailing your principles to the mast at the expense of the play'.

Where it's sensible, where it's not to make a point (like the token casting of some major companies in the eighties) it is progressive. It is something that Donnellan and Ormerod have always championed with their Cheek by Jowl productions. In the broader debate, they have demonstrated that it is possible for theatre to reflect the face of Britain – walk along any high street in Britain and you won't find the colour to be exclusively white, or the voice the RADA-trained Queen's English. And in a Norwegian fantasy, *Peer Gynt*, Donnellan and Ormerod pursued their casting beliefs.

The Olivier is a notoriously problematic stage to fill. Ormerod's large, wooden-slatted, roof-like structure moved about on wheels (more of a strain for the performers to manoeuvre than the lighter pieces of Cheek by Jowl productions). Rotated to become a slope, it was the gentle contours of the fjords where Peer ran in the freedom of his thoughts. It transformed from the rustic homestead of Peer and his mother, by lifting its front, into the grotto of the trolls (with their bottom-heavy, scampering around). This structure dominated the production, showing how home dominated Peer's adventures, making his return to his mother inevitable. 'When we worked in the Olivier,' says Donnellan,

> 'we didn't want to use the revolve, but for the hut to be manipulated by the actors. It's important to empower the actors so that the audience can help them create meaning. Whereas ankle-deep in carpet and faced with a Benson & Hedges advert on the back of your programme, and confronted by all this machinery, the audience can start to lose contact with the actor. The audience might feel permitted to sit back and watch the stage as if it were a television; whereas in theatre, I think, the audience needs to sit forward and make it happen. It's dangerous when the director or the designer take out of the audience's hands that ability to make the play.'

Not everything was as abstractly realised. A sphinx had to be created before rehearsals began for the scenes set in Egypt. A sinking ship was a small model on the horizon, to hilarious comic effect. There were wooden hobby-horses. There was a grille in the stage's floor through which lunatics emerged. These things were concrete. But the Boyg was created by the entire cast, washed in Rick Fisher's green light, and each running a finger around the rim of a glass beaker, creating ethereal, invisible tones. 'The Boyg was a problem,' admits Cunneen:

> 'We didn't know how to do the boyg. I just liked the idea of the sound of forty glasses. They had a big store at the National, so I went down to see what we could come up with. I think it was quite a good sound. I'm not sure that it was the best Boyg that we had – we went through about six options. But I was pleased that it came out of a musical idea. That's what tends to happen. It's not a closed rehearsal process. The thing is very much in a state of flux. It's a form of creative bidding, I suppose, to do with coming up with a good idea'.

Where Peter Stein had had six Peers, Donnellan had two: David Morrisey (who had been in Cheek by Jowl's *Twelfth Night* and *The Cid*) in the first half, in search of abstract self-knowledge and spiritual wealth; and the more mature Stephen Moore in the cynical second half, chasing after material wealth. Michael Billington wrote a neat essay of a review in the *Guardian*, summing up:

> 'Under the mosaic richness we are reminded that Ibsen's attack on individualism (what the Troll King calls "Be true to your self-ish") is as horribly relevant today as it was in 1867' (2/2/90),

and then a further summary in *Country Life* where he considered Donnellan's approach 'radical but true to the spirit of the text' (8/5/90).

There was a cohesion about all the multiple elements of the production. Jane Gibson contributed and shared in a number of those:

> 'We worked on what it's like to live in a grey place with hardly any light. It affects people. And the isolation of the communities means that people aren't near each other physically, but does that strengthen or weaken their emotional bond? I was very aware of the move from *Fuente Ovejuna*, which was hot and Catholic, to *Peer Gynt*, which was cold and Protestant. A different outlook, a different body. You can go very far with that'.

What Donnellan and Ormerod have brought to the National Theatre is their Cheek by Jowl strand of European classics. It's an appropriate home for such work not least because the first real pioneer of this exciting aspect of our contemporary theatre was Kenneth Tynan, as Literary Manager to Olivier's Old Vic. Tynan had been giving informative *Observer* reviews beforehand – championing the Berliner Ensemble when they visited Britain, for example – influencing a wide range of theatre practitioners at the time, an influence that lives on. At the Old Vic, Tynan had the opportunity to practically introduce Britain to a European repertoire, and to European directors: one of his greatest achievements was to secure Ingmar Bergman to direct *Hedda Gabler*. But with a Golden Age of new British writing on the make in the late fifties – sustained throughout the sixties, seventies and early eighties (which many delight in pointing out came once again in an Elizabethan age) – European plays only took firm root in the 1980's. (With the arrival of Robert David Macdonald at the Citizens in the early seventies, there was obviously something Glasgow-ing on. But such work only reached a wider audience through the touring companies in the eighties.) Cheek by Jowl's productions moved the European classic engine up a gear or two – and with the nineties, we are going, excitingly, into overdrive.

Cheek by Jowl's speeding up of the larger vehicle of classics (British and foreign) in Fringe theatre, and their particular style and approach, anticipated the chasm between the Fringe impetus and the classical hiatus in mainstream companies. In joining the National Theatre, the Donnellans and Ormerods have bridged the gap, not jumped the void.

FILM-MAKERS

**'Mother Mary Jesus help us. What kind of thing is that? Is that legs it has? Poor thing, it's so ugly. Your father will eat the face off you'
(Finnuala)**

One wet week in April 1991, a camera crew and production team were on location in the unglamorous semi-detached streets of windy West 5. Impact Pictures, with Ken Russell extravaganzas under its youthful belt, were putting an eleven-minute Channel 4 commission onto celluloid. They filmed by a pond; along suburban hedgerows; and within a dingy Ealing house, which only needed the careful eye of Nick Ormerod, and his Art Director Michael Carlin's tenacity in dressing the set, to take it back to the early sixties of Donnellan's childhood.

The Big Fish is a colourful short film, based on an event in Donnellan's childhood. Donnellan, his younger sister (who, now grown up, arrived during the week of filming to observe) and their parents, had made a home in a staid area of London – the mean spirit of which seemed to be living on in the nineties, as neighbours occasionally flustered the filming, unimpressed, interrupting a scene (and making one) to complain about the disruption of their uneventful weekday afternoons.

As a child, Donnellan had kept a clutter of jam-jars brimming with tadpoles in his tiny bedroom. But, not content with the smallfry of toads, newts and frogs, he headed off into the backstreets of West London, to discover in Hanwell what seemed to him at the time (and amazingly it still exists and features in the film) a secret garden with a pond, with a carp swimming in its murky waters. Equip-ped with a long bamboo pole with net attached and a large plastic carrier bag, he'd caught the fish and brought it home in a taxi. It lived for three days in the bath until his father had a fit of temper and Donnellan dutifully returned the carp to its pond.

It's a tiny incident, one full of the fancies of child-hood. So when David Aukin – who'd left his post as Executive Producer of the National Theatre to become Head of Drama at Channel 4 – invited Ormerod and Donnellan to make a short film for Channel 4's Short & Curlies season, they jumped at the chance to make their film debut by writing the accomplished story of *The Big Fish*.

Their designer-director partnership could almost have been tailor-made for film. *The Big Fish*'s pro-ducer, Jeremy Bolt enthused on location:

'It's exciting to see them bring to cinema the innovation that they've brought to theatre. The script is fantastic, especially by comparison with loads of second-rate screenplays that keep reach-ing the screens. Declan's wonderful with actors, directing the performers much more than most young, first-time directors who are obsessed with the camera shots they've seen in American films. Nick has a terrific eye for the picture, for the cut-ting of shots, for the moods of the exteriors, the atmospheres of the interiors. The double-act works so well. With further camera experience, they'll make a unique and brilliant film team'.

Bolt's praise and admiration was matched by the crew's. They started by being supportive of what was unquestionably a learning experience for Don-nellan and Ormerod, and ended with a keenness and pleasure that they'd been instrumental in transforming these novices into film directors with a future.

There was a kind of poetic justice in the filming process too. Although Donnellan had returned the original carp back to its watery environment in the sixties, the carp who was recreating the role for the nineties escaped in that same pond while filming. Untempted by the career of film-star, the carp's now leading a much happier life as a fish.

EPILOGUE

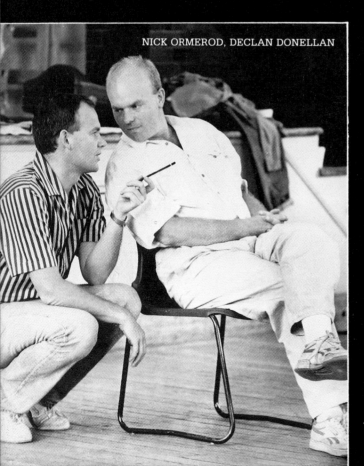

NICK ORMEROD, DECLAN DONELLAN

f there is one company that can be said to have influenced British theatre in the Eighties it is Cheek by Jowl. There is not a fringe production of a classic play anywhere that does not have a whiff of the company's spirited iconoclasm (Alex Renton *Independent* 11/1/89)

Most involved in theatre will summon up the ghosts of past productions, of legendary playwrights, of an age of subsidy and the right to fail, when theatre changed people's lives and philosophies. Hankering after such a hope, those born in the sixties dutifully read their Edgars, Brentons, Hares, Bonds, Churchills and Ardens (John, not the Shakespeare editions) and do their best to re-create Brook's *Dream* in their mind's eye.

The 1980's were their formative years: the time of media not marijuana, the age of the *Independent* not the *Manchester Guardian*. And yet they still choose to work in theatre, to observe it, to write about it. What kept their passions going? What prevented them from following the footsteps of their contemporaries? Why didn't they get that proper job in the media? Why could theatre still thrill them?

Many will mention specific productions, playwrights, actors, or one-off experiences in the theatre. Others will say it was in Mime, or in Europe, or in Opera where their imaginations were stirred. Others will claim that the lack of anything truly invigorating convinced them that only they could offer it to a dwindling theatrical culture. Some might possibly say: 'Cheek by Jowl'.

If Cheek by Jowl and its work really was the best of a decade of theatre, then what does that say about that decade? Cynics could easily debunk Cheek by Jowl's merits and worth, and reflect upon what 1980's theatre failed to offer. It would be easy to pour scorn upon the context of Cheek by Jowl and thus, by implication, belittle Cheek by Jowl too. One could be extremely cynical and claim that the success is relative in a decade where gimpish audience tastes and theatrical effects substituted challenging drama; a dire slump in state funding closed some innovative and radical companies and only enhanced gargantuan institutions; and private money and celebrity status provoked a fast-buck West End show or a coy Renaissance.

If Cheek by Jowl has been dictated to by fashion – a malaise with new writing necessitating, and a mood in society informing the situation where we turn to what we might perceive as the reassurance of classical work – then it is only because they have created that fashion themselves.

Classic reinterpretation became sexy in the eighties, starry and glamorous. If it upset the fundamentalists when it seemed subversive, that's no mean feat in the decade of the SDP. But it wasn't truly subversive – the practitioners adored their material. The production of a play shouldn't bother us if it's not how we remember the text, for theatre should please as theatre, not as a servitor to a literary tradition.

Cheek by Jowl at any time would impress. Their theatre is a communal and intelligent celebration in orthodox playhouses. It is the major company of the 1980's and beyond to have consistently – and that's the key feature – produced work which struck many as innovative, ground-breaking, pioneering, and happily inspired many more. It would be difficult to find another single subject within the 1980's alone that one could commend – easier to gather together a series of one-off plays and productions presented by a hotchpotch of managements.

Cheek by Jowl was part of a burgeoning movement for European classics as part of the British repertoire (though no one would claim their six foreign plays led this movement single-handedly). They knocked sense into Shakespeare sometimes by excessive nonsense, but always refreshing in comparison to institutionalised, tired productions. They epitomise the recognition that there is an eager audience for theatre far beyond London. Not everyone likes all their work. Some like none. But that's healthy, for it demonstrates that tastes aren't singular or broadly fashionable.

If you acknowledge the pitfalls of the context in which Cheek by Jowl flourished, you still recognise that they flourished. Cheek by Jowl has shared with us ten years of theatrical celebration. The party's not over yet.

APPENDICES

The first £6,000 for the *Country Wife* tour (with an extra £1,154 from the Scottish Arts Council) in exchange for 49 performances, came as project funding from the Touring Department, even though the application had been made to the Drama Department. A recurring feature of Cheek by Jowl's funding is the fluctuation between these two departments as the Arts Council have tried to sort out how Cheek by Jowl fits into its guidelines – it's either to the credit of the Arts Council, or the lack of compromise by Cheek by Jowl, that the Arts Council congratulate the company on teaching them to be flexible.

Othello received £10,000 for 79 performances on its first Autumn tour; the Arts Council advised against Cheek by Jowl becoming an Equity company at this stage – obliging them to pay the actors and stage managers the union rates – since the funding wasn't quite enough to cover it. Matthews' meticulous accounting meant that there was enough left over from this grant to finance the Spring tour (an application for additional funds was turned down, the only time in Cheek by Jowl's history). The actors were paid £85 per week.

During the tour of *Vanity Fair*, Cheek by Jowl were able to become an Equity company, paying their employees £110 per week. The £22,000 awarded by the Touring Department (again the application was made to Drama) was to give 85 performances, the projects obviously growing in size. For a smaller tour, which included *Pericles*, an additional £15,000 was awarded. And then the

Andromache/Vanity Fair/Pericles tour was offered £35,000 – though only £29,441 was taken. Curiously, part of this grant was paid to the company before it had even been officially decided that they were to receive a grant at all:

'It has been agreed to offer an advance of £17,000 on subsidy yet to be awarded'.

For a ten week Spring 1986 tour of *A Midsummer Night's Dream*, £17,000 was given to Cheek by Jowl. By the end of the first *Midsummer Night's Dream* tour, Cheek by Jowl felt that they had formed a company of core actors, a virtual long-term ensemble which has always been their ideal, and after their exciting experiences as a cohesive troupe with the trio of plays, they launched themselves into researching and devising a Second World War epic, *Bulldog Breed*. The tour was booked – but cancelled after two weeks work (during which £84 of Arts Council money had been spent) with *The Man of Mode* taking its place, touring alongside a re-cast *Midsummer Night's Dream*. For that Autumn tour, the Arts Council granted £29,000.

For 26 weeks and 73 performances from 1986–1987, *Twelfth Night* and *The Cid* received £80,000. This grant was significant because it indicated that Cheek by Jowl were being treated as a *de facto* annual client, with the money awarded 'for the year ending March 1987'. It wasn't strictly a revenue grant, but nor was it a project grant either. Perhaps it was because Cheek by Jowl were planning further ahead that it seemed expedient for the Arts Council to demonstrate their commitment to a flagship, small-scale touring company by awarding grants on this yearly basis (as opposed to grants for specific tours).

In the financial year 1987–1988, the paperwork for Matthews was finally reduced as Cheek by Jowl became an annual client *de jure*, a grant of £105,000 awarded to tour the small-scale venue circuit. In addition, a project grant of an extra £29,500 was made available for an eight week, middle-scale tour of *Macbeth* (a co-production with York Theatre Royal), the Arts Council acknowledging Cheek by Jowl's potential and ambitions to move to a middle-scale touring circuit. This middle-scale money was made available through a development fund, even though Cheek by Jowl didn't actually fall into any of the Arts Council's priority areas.

In 1988–1989 £107,000 came from the Drama Department, for the first time, with another project fund award of £29,500 for *The Tempest*. The middle-scale work of Cheek by Jowl was being recognised without being officially consolidated. This odd attitude became crystal clear when in 1989–1990, within the £139,140, £30,000 was included for touring,

'but should not be regarded as part of your company's base-line subsidy',

even though that money had effectively been an additional part of a base-line subsidy for three years in a row.

The LWT prize of £15,000 had financed *Philoctetes*. The guest artistic team of Lindsay Posner and Julian McGowan was brought in to direct *The Doctor of Honour*. *Sara* was postponed for the financial year which produced *Lady Betty*, to join *Hamlet* for the year 1990–1991, when Cheek by Jowl received £116,000.

Cheek by Jowl, together with Century Theatre, was the first revenue client of the Arts Council Touring Department. That department understandably didn't feel that it was appropriate to set up an appraisal system for only two such companies, so the responsibility for funding was transferred to the Drama Department (in 1988). The advantage of this was that the money could be used to cover a London run (London runs were strictly outside the Touring Department's orbit, and companies had to go it alone). With profits made from London runs anyway, it was merely a pleasing reassurance for Cheek by Jowl.

The £90,000 awarded for 1991–1992 in exchange for only seven weeks touring at Arts Council approved venues (Cheek by Jowl will obviously spend longer on the road than this, especially with their international engagements) is a clear acceptance by the Arts Council of Cheek by Jowl's wish to do one tour not two. Up until this financial year, Cheek by Jowl received its annual grant for one middle-scale tour and one small-scale tour. With the growth in artistic ambition, Cheek by Jowl now prefer to drop their small-scale touring, and *As You Like It* is indicative of their full maturity as middle-scale play producers.

1981 · THE COUNTRY WIFE by Wycherley
Horner · Kevin Burke
Harcourt/Mistress Squeamish · Michael Irwin
Sparkish · Nigel Leach
Pinchwife · Simon Needs
Alithea/Lady Fidget · Jane Maud
Sir Jasper Fidget/Margery · Caroline Swift

Director · Declan Donnellan
Designer · Nick Ormerod
Stage Manager · Caroline Donnellan

1982 · GOTCHA by Barrie Keefe
Ton · Michael Rigg
Lynne · Leda Hodgson
Kid · Gareth Kirkland
Head · Peter Kinsey

Director · Declan Donnellan
Designer · Nick Ormerod
Company Stage Manager · Martin Coates
Deputy Stage Manager · Sandra Ball

1982 · RACK ABBEY by Declan Donnellan & Colin Sell
Gherkin · Gareth Kirkland
Pinkerton-Forbes · Peter Kinsey
Noreen/Mother/Matron/Smiley · Leda Hodgson
Smethwick/Father/Mr Kent · Michael Rigg

Director · Declan Donnellan
Designer · Nick Ormerod
Company Stage Manager · Martin Coates
Deputy Stage Manager · Sandra Ball

1982 · OTHELLO by Shakespeare
Roderigo/Officer · Kevin Huckstep (then Michael Rigg)
Iago · Geoffrey Morgan (then Gene Foad)
Brabantio/Montano/Lodovico · Peter Broad (then Tony Chambers)
Othello · Doyle Richmond (then Ruddy L. Davis)
Cassio · Andrew Collins
Doge/Emilia · Barbara Brann (then Anne White)
Desdemona/Bianca · Amanda Harris

Director · Declan Donnellan
Designer · Nick Ormerod
Original Music & Musical Direction · Colin Sell
Wardrobe Supervisor · Christine Meddison (then Kim Kenny)
Fight Director · John Waller
Stage Manager · James Unvala
Assistant Stage Manager · Sandra Ball

1983 · VANITY FAIR by Thackeray, adapted by Declan Donnellan & Nick Ormerod
Miss Pinkerton,Mr Sedley,Rawdon Crawley,
Isidor,Miss Glorvina O'Dowd · Andrew Collins
Jemima Pinkerton,Joseph Sedley,
Mr Osborne,Raggles · Martin Turner
Amelia Sedley,Mrs Raggles · Amanda Harris
Rebecca Sharp · Sadie Shimmin
George Osborne,Sir Pitt Crawley,Marquis of Steyne · Duncan Bell
William Dobbin,Pitt Crawley,Pauline,
Lord Southdown,Correspondent · Simon Dormandy
Mrs Sedley,Miss Crawley,Mrs Major O'Dowd,
Marchioness of Steyne · Anne White

Director · Declan Donnellan
Designer · Nick Ormerod
Score & Musical Direction · Jeremy Sams
Company Stage Manager · Nick Kidd
Costumes · Kim Kenny

1984 · PERICLES by Shakespeare
Antiochus/2nd Fisherman/3rd Knight
Philemon/Leonine/Lysimachus · Simon Dormandy
Antiochus' Daughter/3rd Fisherman
2nd Knight/Marina · Amanda Harris
Perides/1st Pirate/1st Gentleman · Andrew Collins

Helicanus/Simonides/2nd Sailor/3rd Pirate
Pander/2nd Gentleman · Martin Turner
Cleon/1st Fisherman/1st Knight/1st Sailor
Cerimon/2nd Priate/Boult · Duncan Bell
Dionyza/Thaisa · Sadie Shimmin
Lychorida/Ephesian Lady/Bawd/Goddess Diana · Deirdre Edwards

Director · Declan Donnallan
Designer · Nick Ormerod
Music · James Antony Ellis
Choreography · Sara van Beers
Company Stage Manager · Nick Kidd
Costumes made by · Charlotte Humpston
Company Movement · Ilan Reichel
Company Voice · Charmian Hoare

1984 · ANDROMACHE by Racine, translated by David Bryer
Orestes · Andrew Collins
Pylades · Simon Dormandy
Pyrrhus · Duncan Bell
Phoenix · Martin Turner
Hermione · Sadie Shimmin
Cleone · Deirdre Edwards
Andromache · Amanda Harris
Cephisa · Anne White

Director · Declan Donnellan
Set Designer · Nick Ormerod
Costume Designers · Kim Kenny & Nick Ormerod
Company Stage Manager · Nick Kidd
Company Movement · Ilan Reichel
Company Voice · Charmian Hoare

1985 · A MIDSUMMER NIGHT'S DREAM by Shakespeare
Hippolyta/Titania · Anne White
Theseus/Oberon · Duncan Bell (then Martin Turner)
Philostrate/Puck · David Gillespie
Hermia · Saskia Reeves
Egeus/Mr (Rev) Bottom · Simon Dormandy (then Colin Wakefield)
Lysander · Martin Turner (then Paul Sykes)
Demetrius · Colin Wakefield (then William Chubb)
Helena · Claire Vousden (then Sally Greenwood)
Miss Quince · Steph Bramwell
Miss Flute · Leda Hodgson

Director · Declan Donnellan
Designer · Nick Ormerod
Lighting Design · Nick Kidd
Choreographer · Sara van Beers
Director's Assistant · Karen Ballard (then Lindsay Posner)
Company Stage Manager · Nick Kidd (then Clare Le May)
Costumes by · Charlotte Humpston
Company Voice · Patsy Rodenburg

1985 · THE MAN OF MODE by Etherege
Mr Dorimant · Martin Turner
Handy/Old Bellair · Colin Wakefield
Foggy Nan/Lady Woodvil · Steph Bramwell
Mr Medley · William Chubb
Young Bellair · Paul Sykes
Lady Townley/Mrs Loveit · Anne White
Emilia/Pert · Sally Greenwood
Bellinda/Busy · Leda Hodgson
Harriet · Saskia Reeves
Sir Fopling Flutter/Mr Smirk · David Gillespie

Director · Declan Donnellan
Designer · Nick Ormerod
Assistant Director · Lindsay Posner
Music · Joanna MacGregor
Choreographer · Sara van Beers
Lighting Design/Company Stage Manager · Nick Kidd
Assistant Stage Manager · Clare Le May
Costume Supervisor · Lorraine Naylor
Company Voice · Patsy Rodenburg

1986 · **TWELFTH NIGHT by Shakespeare**
    Viola · Patricia Kerrigan (then Clare Hackett)
    Sebastian · David Morrissey (then Lloyd Owen)
    Antonio · Patrick Romer (then Robert Merry)
    Sea Captain/Sir Toby Belch · Keith Bartlett
    Orsino · Timothy Walker

    Curio · Alex Starr (then Tom Skippings)
    Olivia · Anne White
    Malvolio · Hugh Ross
    Valentine · Aden Gillett (then Tom Skippings)
    Sir Andrew Aguecheek · Aden Gillett (then Michael Jenn)
    Maria · Melinda McGraw (then Jiggy Bhore)
    Feste · Stephen Simms (then Guy Henry)
    Director · Declan Donnellan
    Designer · Nick Ormerod
    Composer/Musical Director · Joanna MacGregor
    Choreographer · Sara van Beers
    Stage Manager/Lighting Designer · Alex Starr
    Assistant Stage Manager · Mary Askham (then Garry Strater)
    Costume Supervisor · Louise Page

1986 · **THE CID by Corneille, translated by David Bryer**
    Elvira · Mary Askham
    Don Gomez · Keith Bartlett
    Chimena · Patricia Kerrigan
    The Infanta · Anne White
    Leonora · Melinda McGraw
    Don Diego · Patrick Romer
    Don Rodrigo · Aden Gillett
    Don Arias · Stephen Simms
    Don Alonzo · David Morrissey
    The King · Hugh Ross
    Don Sancho · Timothy Walker

    Director · Declan Donnellan
    Designer · Nick Ormerod
    Composer/Musical Director · Joanna MacGregor
    Stage Manager/Lighting Designer · Alex Starr
    Costume Supervisor · Louise Page

1987 · **MACBETH by Shakespeare**
    Duncan/Macduff · Des McAleer (then Martin Turner)
    Malcolm · Timothy Walker
    Donalbain/1st Murderer · Lloyd Owen
    Sergeant/2nd Murderer · Ged McKenna
    Lennox · Anthony Dixon
    Ross · Liam Halligan
    Macbeth · Keith Bartlett
    Banquo/Doctor · Raymond Sawyer
    Angus · Duncan Duff
    Lady Macbeth · Leslee Udwin
    Fleance/Young Macduff · Simon Bolton
    Porter/Lady Macduff · Anne White

    Director · Declan Donnellan
    Designer · Nick Ormerod
    Lighting Designers · Nick Kidd & Nick Ormerod
    Company Stage Manager · Garry Straker
    Technical Stage Manager · Nick Kidd
    Deputy Stage Manager · Shona Penman
    Fight Director · John Waller
    Dialect Coach · Joan Washington

1988 · **A FAMILY AFFAIR by Ostrovsky, in a new version by Nick Dear**
    Lipochka · Lesley Sharp
    Agrafena · Anne White
    Fominishna · Annette Badland
    Ustinya · Marcia Warren
    Rispolozhensky · Timothy Walker
    Bolshov · Tam Dean Burn
    Lazar · Adam Kotz
    Tishka · Paul Stacey

    Director · Declan Donnellan
    Designer · Nick Ormerod
    Music Director · Colin Sell
    Lighting Designer/Technical Stage Manager · Nick Kidd
    Choreographer · Anne Browne
    Company Stage Manager · Garry Straker
    Wardrobe Mistress · Theresa Keating
    Costume Supervisor · Louise Page

1988 · **PHILOCTETES by Sophocles, translated by Kenneth McLeish**
    Odysseus · Charlie Roe
    Neoptolemos · Paterson Joseph
    Philoctetes · Keith Bartlett
    A Merchant · Trevor Baxter
    Heracles · Duncan Duff
    Neoptolemos' Sailors · Peter Darling, Duncan Duff, Michael Jenn, Lloyd Owen, Cecilia Noble, Dale Rapley, Timothy Walker

    Director · Declan Donnellan
    Designer · Nick Ormerod
    Composer/Music Director · Paddy Cunneen
    Lighting Designer · Steve Rate
    Assistant to the Director · Anne White
    Company Stage Manager · Garry Straker
    Stage Managers · Shona Penman & Steve Rate
    Voice · Patsy Rodenburg
    Costume Supervision · Louise Page

1988 · **THE TEMPEST by Shakespeare**
    Prospero · Timothy Walker
    Miranda · Cecilia Noble
    Antonio · Charlie Roe
    The Queen of Naples · Anne White
    Ferdinand · Lloyd Owen
    Sebastian · Dale Rapley
    Gonzalo · Trevor Baxter
    Adrian · Paterson Joseph
    Stephano · Keith Bartlett
    Trinculo · Michael Jenn
    Ariel · Peter Darling
    Caliban · Duncan Duff

    Director · Declan Donnellan
    Designer · Nick Ormerod
    Composer/Music Director · Paddy Cunneen
    Lighting Designers · Nicker Ormerod & Steve Rate
    Assistant Director · Declan Hughes
    Choreographer · Sara van Beers
    Company Stage Manager · Garry Straker
    Stage Managers · Shona Penman & Steve Rate
    Voice · Patsy Rodenburg
    Costume Supervision · Louise Page

1989 · **THE DOCTOR OF HONOUR by Calderon, translated by Roy Campbell**
    Don Pedro · William Hope
    Don Henry · Neil Pearson
    Don Gutierre · Nigel Terry
    Don Arias/Ludovico · Kilian McKenna
    Don Diego · Ben Onwukwe
    Dona Mencia · Michelle Fairley
    Dona Leonor · Claire Benedict
    Coquin · Mark Williams
    Jacinta · Sue Devaney

    Director · Lindsay Posner
    Designer · Julian McGowan
    Music Director · Stephen Warbeck
    Lighting Designer · Rick Fisher
    Company Stage Manager · Hazel Ryan
    Deputy Stage Manager · Charles Carne
    Costume Supervisor · Louise Page
    Movement Consultant · Geraldine Stephenson

1989 · **LADY BETTY by Declan Donnellan, music by Paddy Cunneen**
    Betty · Sally Dexter

John/Oliver/Captain Mills · Tim McMullan
Sarah/Morning · Lucy Tregear
Father Molloy/Michael Flynn · Gerard O'Hare
Night/Bridie O'Byrne · Catherine White
Silence/George/Rev Blakeney · Lawrence Evans
Cold/Liamog Hanrahan · Phil McKee
O'Leary/Liam Hanrahan · Ray McBride
Mrs Mills/Peggy Hanrahan · Charlotte Medcalf
Dunne/Christie O'Flaherty · Patrick Toomey

Director · Declan Donnellan
Designer · Nick Ormerod
Music · Paddy Cunneen
Movement Director · Jane Gibson
Lighting Designer · Ben Ormerod
Company Stage Manager · Louise Yeomans
Technical Stage Manager · Charles Carne
Deputy Stage Manager · Martin Lloyd-Evans
Wardrobe Mistress · Blossom Beale
Costume Supervisor · Angie Burns
Dialect Coach · Sally Grace

Preliminary work on *Lady Betty* took place at the National
Theatre Studio with: Mark Addy, Toby Byrne, Mary Chater,
Peter Collyer, Jo Stone Fewings, Leona Heimfield, Melee
Hutton, Rachel Joyce, Paul McCleary, Peter Nicholas,
Tim Payne, Clive Rowe, Trevor Sellars.

1990 · SARA by Lessing, translated by Ernest Bell
Sir William Sampson · Daniel Thorndike
Waitwell · Peter Needham
Landlord of an inn · Max Burrows
Mellefont · Raad Rawi
Norton · Duncan Duff
Betty · Charlotte Medcalf
Sara Sampson · Rachel Joyce
Marwood · Sheila Gish
Hannah · Pat O'Toole
Arabella · Maria Isabel Hernandez

Director · Declan Donnellan
Designer · Nick Ormerod
Music Director · Paddy Cunneen
Movement Director · Jane Gibson
Lighting Designer · Rick Fisher
Company Stage Manager · Louise Yeomans
Deputy Stage Manager · Martin Lloyd-Evans
Student Stage Manager · Paul Clay
Touring Electrician · Judith Greenwood
Wardrobe Mistress · Christine Maddison
Wardrobe Supervisor · Angie Burns
Voice Coach · Patsy Rodenburg

1990 · HAMLET by Shakespeare
Barnardo/Guildenstern/Priest · Malcolm Scates
Francisco/Reynaldo/Player Queen/Fortinbras · Peter Moreton
Marcellus/Rosencrantz · Patrick Miller
Horatio · Duncan Duff
Hamlet's Ghost/Player King/2nd Gravedigger · Daniel Thorndike
Claudius · Scott Cherry
Voltemand/Captain/Messenger/Osric · Jason Morell
Laertes · Peter de Jersey
Polonius/1st Gravedigger · Peter Needham
Hamlet · Timothy Walker
Gertrude · Natasha Parry
Ophelia · Cathryn Bradshaw

Director · Declan Donnellan
Designer · Nick Ormerod
Composer/Music Director · Paddy Cunneen
Movement Director · Jane Gibson
Lighting Designers · Rick Fisher & Judith Greenwood
Fight Director · John Waller
Company Stage Manager · Louise Yeomans
Deputy Stage Manager · Martin Lloyd Evans
Assistant Stage Manager · Paul Clay

Wardrobe Managers · Blossom Beale (then Amanda Dawes)
Wardrobe Supervisor · Angie Burns

1991 · AS YOU LIKE IT by Shakespeare
Corin/Le Beau · Mike Afford
Oliver · Mark Bannister
Silvius · Mark Benton
Audrey · Richard Cant
Jaques/Charles · Joe Dixon
Phebe/Adam · Sam Graham
Jacques du Boys/1st Lord · Richard Henders
The Dukes · David Hobbs
Celia · Tom Hollander
Dennis/Sir Oliver Martext/2nd Lord · Anthony Hunt
Rosalind · Adrian Lester
Touchstone · Peter Needham
Amiens/Hymen · Conrad Nelson
Orlando · Patrick Toomey

Director · Declan Donnellan
Designer · Nick Ormerod
Composer/MD · Paddy Cunneen
Lighting Designer · Judith Greenwood
Movement Director · Sue Lefton
Fight Director · John Waller
Production & Company Stage Manager · Louise Yeomans
Deputy Stage Manager · Maria Gibbons
Student Assistant Stage Manager · Andrea Hopkinson
Wardrobe Manager · Blossom Beale

ADMINISTRATIVE STAFF

Administrative Director · Barbara Matthews 1981—present

Assistant Administrators · Richard Hansom 1985
· Edel Musselle 1987—1988
· Deborah Aydon 1988—1989
· Jill Hunter 1989—1990
· Maria Evans 1990—present

PR & Marketing Officers · Elaine McGowan 1988—1989
· Ruth Ingledow 1990—present

Since the Donmar Warehouse run of *Vanity Fair, Pericles*
and *Andromache* in 1985,
Sharon Kean has been Cheek by Jowl's London
season's Press Representative

Since *Vanity Fair* in 1983, Iain Lanyon has been the
Graphic Designer for Cheek by Jowl

Aberdeen
Vanity Fair
Accrington
Vanity Fair
Adelaide
As You Like It
Aldeburgh
Othello
Aldershot
The Country Wife Vanity Fair Pericles
Alexandria
A Midsummer Night's Dream
Alkmaar
Gotcha & Rack Abbey
Almagro
Pericles
Ambleside
Othello Vanity Fair
Amersfoort
Gotcha & Rack Abbey
Amiens
Twelfth Night
Amstelveen
Gotcha & Rack Abbey
Amsterdam
Gotcha & Rack Abbey
Ankara
Twelfth Night The Tempest Philoctetes
Antwerp
Gotcha & Rack Abbey
Apeldoorn
Gotcha & Rack Abbey
Armagh
Vanity Fair
Arnhem
Gotcha & Rack Abbey
Assen
Gotcha & Rack Abbey
Athens
Hamlet
Averham
Vanity Fair
Aylesbury
Vanity Fair A Midsummer Night's Dream

Bacup
Pericles
Banbury
Vanity Fair
Bangalore
A Midsummer Night's Dream
Bangor
Othello Vanity Fair
Barcelona
A Midsummer Night's Dream As You Like It
Barrow
Othello Vanity Fair
Barton-on-Humber
Vanity Fair Pericles
Basildon
Othello Vanity Fair A Midsummer Night's Dream
The Tempest Philoctetes Lady Betty Hamlet
Basingstoke
Othello Vanity Fair Pericles The Cid A Family Affair
The Doctor of Honour
Belfast
As You Like It
Biggar
Othello Vanity Fair
Billericay
Vanity Fair
Birmingham
The Country Wife Twelfth Night The Cid
A Family Affair The Doctor of Honour

Bombay
A Midsummer Night's Dream
Boston
Vanity Fair Twelfth Night
Bourges
Twelfth Night
Bourne End
A Midsummer Night's Dream
Bracknell
Vanity Fair Pericles Twelfth Night The Cid The Tempest
Philoctetes Lady Betty Hamlet As You Like It
Bratislava
The Tempest Philoctetes
Brasilia
A Midsummer Night's Dream As You Like It
Breda
Gotcha & Rack Abbey
Bridgnorth
Othello Vanity Fair A Midsummer Night's Dream
Bridgwater
Vanity Fair
Brighton
Twelfth Night The Cid Macbeth The Tempest Philoctetes
Broadstairs
Pericles
Bronte
A Midsummer Night's Dream
Brussels
Gotcha & Rack Abbey
Bucharest
The Tempest Philoctetes
Buckingham
Othello
Builth Wells
A Midsummer Night's Dream A Family Affair The Doctor of Honour
Burton on Trent
Vanity Fair Pericles Andromache A Midsummer Night's Dream
The Man of Mode
Bury St Edmunds
Vanity Fair Pericles A Midsummer Night's Dream
The Man of Mode Twelfth Night The Cid Macbeth
A Family Affair Lady Betty Sara Hamlet As You Like It
Buxton
Andromache A Midsummer Night's Dream
Twelfth Night As You Like It

Cairo
A Midsummer Night's Dream
Calcutta
A Midsummer Night's Dream
Cambridge
Twelfth Night The Cid Macbeth A Family Affair The Tempest
Philoctetes Lady Betty Sara Hamlet As You Like It
Canterbury
Vanity Fair Pericles Andromache The Cid
Carlisle
Othello A Midsummer Night's Dream Twelfth Night
The Cid A Family Affair
Chertsey
Vanity Fair
Chipping Norton
The Country Wife Vanity Fair Andromache
The Man of Mode The Cid The Doctor of Honour
Cleethorpes
A Midsummer Night's Dream
Colchester
Vanity Fair A Family Affair
Coleraine
Vanity Fair Pericles Andromache
Cologne
Vanity Fair Pericles
Colombo
A Midsummer Night's Dream

Copenhagen
Twelfth Night
Coventry
The Tempest Philoctetes Sara Hamlet As You Like It
Crawley
The Doctor of Honour
Crewe
Othello
Croydon
Pericles
Cuyk
Gotcha & Rack Abbey

Dartington
Othello Vanity Fair
Delhi
A Midsummer Night's Dream
Den Haag
Gotcha & Rack Abbey
Dhaka
A Midsummer Night's Dream
Dilbeek
Gotcha & Rack Abbey
Doetincham
Gotcha & Rack Abbey
Drachten
Gotcha & Rack Abbey
Dublin
Twelfth Night The Cid As You Like It
Dudley
The Country Wife
Dumfries
Othello
Dundee
The Country Wife
Durham
Vanity Fair
Dusseldorf
Vanity Fair

Eastbourne
Vanity Fair A Midsummer Night's Dream The Man of Mode
Edinburgh
The Country Wife Vanity Fair
Ellesmere
The Country Wife Vanity Fair Pericles
Epsom
Vanity Fair Pericles Andromache A Midsummer Night's Dream
Twelfth Night The Doctor of Honour
Erlangen
Vanity Fair Pericles
Evesham
Othello Vanity Fair
Exeter
A Midsummer Night's Dream

Fareham
Othello Vanity Fair Pericles Andromache The Cid
The Doctor of Honour
Farnham
As You Like It
Frome
Vanity Fair Pericles

Gainsborough
Vanity Fair
Gatehouse
Vanity Fair
Glasgow
Vanity Fair Andromache
Gorinchem
Gotcha & Rack Abbey
Grimsby
Vanity Fair Pericles

Groningen
Gotcha & Rack Abbey
Great Yarmouth
Vanity Fair
Guildford
The Country Wife Vanity Fair
Gutersloh
Pericles
Haaksbergen
Gotcha & Rack Abbey
Haarlem
Gotcha & Rack Abbey
Haifa
Vanity Fair
Halesowen
Othello Vanity Fair
Harderwijk
Gotcha & Rack Abbey
Harlow
A Family Affair
Hasselt
Gotcha & Rack Abbey
Heerlen
Gotcha & Rack Abbey
Helmond
Gotcha & Rack Abbey
Helsinki
Twelfth Night
Hemel Hempstead
Vanity Fair Pericles Andromache A Midsummer Night's Dream
The Man of Mode The Cid A Family Affair The Doctor of Honour
Hereford
The Country Wife Othello Vanity Fair Pericles Twelfth Night
Heusden-Zolder
Gotcha & Rack Abbey
High Wycombe
Vanity Fair
Hilversum
Gotcha & Rack Abbey
Hong Kong
Hamlet
Hoogeveen
Gotcha & Rack Abbey
Hoorn
Gotcha & Rack Abbey
Horsham
The Country Wife Hamlet
Hounslow
The Doctor of Honour
Huddersfield
The Country Wife
Hull
A Midsummer Night's Dream The Man of Mode Twelfth Night The Cid

Ipswich
A Midsummer Night's Dream Twelfth Night
Irvine
Othello Vanity Fair Pericles

Islamabad
A Midsummer Night's Dream
Istanbul
Twelfth Night The Tempest Philoctetes

Jerusalem
Vanity Fair Pericles

Kandy
A Midsummer Night's Dream
Karachi
A Midsummer Night's Dream
Keswick
Othello
Kathmandu
A Midsummer Night's Dream

Kidderminster
The Country Wife Othello Vanity Fair Pericles
Twelfth Night The Doctor of Honour
King's Lynn
Othello Vanity Fair Pericles Andromache
A Midsummer Night's Dream
The Man of Mode The Cid The Doctor of Honour
Kircudbright
Othello
Kotrijk
Gotcha & Rack Abbey
Kuala Lumpur
The Tempest
Kyoto
Hamlet

Lahore
A Midsummer Night's Dream
Lancaster
Othello
Langholm
Vanity Fair
Leeuwarden
Gotcha & Rack Abbey
Leicester
Vanity Fair
Leiden
Gotcha & Rack Abbey
Leighton Buzzard
A Midsummer Night's Dream The Doctor of Honour
Lichfield
A Midsummer Night's Dream The Man of Mode
Liverpool
Twelfth Night
Llantwit Major
A Midsummer Night's Dream
Lochgelly
Othello
London
The Country Wife Othello Vanity Fair Pericles
Andromache A Midsummer Night's Dream The Man of Mode
Twelfth Night The Cid Macbeth A Family Affair
The Tempest Philoctetes The Doctor of Honour
Lady Betty Sara Hamlet As You Like It
Loughborough
Andromache
Louth
Vanity Fair Pericles A Midsummer Night's Dream
Lowestoft
A Midsummer Night's Dream The Man of Mode The Cid
Ludwigshafen
Pericles
Luton
Vanity Fair A Midsummer Night's Dream
The Man of Mode Twelfth Night
Luxembourg
As You Like It

Maastricht
Gotcha & Rack Abbey
Madras
A Midsummer Night's Dream
Madrid
Pericles
Maidstone
Vanity Fair
Market Drayton
The Country Wife
Meppel
Gotcha & Rack Abbey
Milton Keynes
Vanity Fair A Midsummer Night's Dream The Man of Mode
Twelfth Night The Cid A Family Affair

Moffat
Othello
Montevideo
A Midsummer Night's Dream Sara
Munich
Vanity Fair Pericles Twelfth Night

Neerpelt
Gotcha & Rack Abbey
Nelson
The Country Wife
Newtown
A Midsummer Night's Dream The Man of Mode
Nijmegen
Gotcha & Rack Abbey
Norwich
Vanity Fair Pericles Andromache
A Midsummer Night's Dream The Man of Mode

Oldham
The Country Wife
Omagh
Vanity Fair
Ormskirk
Vanity Fair
Oslo
Twelfth Night The Tempest Philoctetes
Oswestry
Othello Andromache A Midsummer Night's Dream The Man of Mode
Oundle
Vanity Fair A Midsummer Night's Dream Twelfth Night
The Cid A Family Affair The Doctor of Honour
Oxford
The Country Wife

Pendley
Vanity Fair Pericles
Perth
The Tempest Philoctetes
Peshawar
A Midsummer Night's Dream
Plovdiv
Twelfth Night
Plymouth
The Country Wife Othello Vanity Fair Pericles
Porto Alegre
A Midsummer Night's Dream
Portsmouth
Pericles
Prague
The Tempest Philoctetes
Preston
A Midsummer Night's Dream
Princes Risborough
Othello

Recife
A Midsummer Night's Dream As You Like It
Redhill
Macbeth
Richmond
A Midsummer Night's Dream The Cid
Rio de Janiero
A Midsummer Night's Dream As You Like It
Roermond
Gotcha & Rack Abbey
Roosendaal
Gotcha & Rack Abbey
Rotterdam
Gotcha & Rack Abbey
Rugby
The Country Wife Othello Vanity Fair Pericles Andromache
A Midsummer Night's Dream The Man of Mode
Runcorn
Vanity Fair

St Andrews
The Country Wife
St Austell
Vanity Fair
Sao Paulo
A Midsummer Night's Dream As You Like It
Scunthorpe
Vanity Fair Macbeth Lady Betty
Shrewsbury
Othello Vanity Fair Andromache A Midsummer Night's Dream
The Man of Mode Twelfth Night
Singapore
The Tempest Philoctetes
Sittard
Gotcha & Rack Abbey
Skegness
Vanity Fair
Sophia
Twelfth Night
Southport
Vanity Fair Pericles
Stadskanaal
Gotcha & Rack Abbey
Stafford
Othello Vanity Fair A Family Affair
Stamford
Vanity Fair Pericles Twelfth Night The Cid
Stevenage
Vanity Fair
Stirling
The Country Wife
Stoke on Trent
Vanity Fair
Stoney Brook
As You Like It
Stranraer
Othello Vanity Fair
Strasbourg
A Midsummer Night's Dream
Stratford upon Avon
Twelfth Night The Cid A Family Affair The Tempest
Philoctetes The Doctor of Honour As You Like It
Stratton on Fosse
The Country Wife
Strombeek-Bever
Gotcha & Rack Abbey
Sudbury
Vanity Fair A Midsummer Night's Dream The Man of Mode
Sutton
Vanity Fair

Tampere
Twelfth Night
Tamworth
Othello Vanity Fair
Taormina
A Midsummer Night's Dream Twelfth Night The Tempest Philoctetes
Taunton
The Tempest Philoctetes Lady Betty Hamlet
Telford
Othello
Tewkesbury
 A Midsummer Night's Dream Twelfth Night
Thame
A Midsummer Night's Dream
Thesaloniki
Hamlet
Thornhill
Vanity Fair
Tokyo
Hamlet As You Like It
Tolworth
Pericles

Torrington
Vanity Fair
Tunbridge Wells
Vanity Fair Pericles The Doctor of Honour
Turnhout
The Tempest Philoctetes

Uppingham
The Country Wife Othello Vanity Fair

Valladolid
Pericles

Wakefield
Macbeth
Wallingford
Vanity Fair A Midsummer Night's Dream
A Family Affair The Doctor of Honour
Warminster
Vanity Fair
Warsaw
Twelfth Night
Washington
Vanity Fair
Wellington
As You Like It
Wells
A Midsummer Night's Dream The Man of Mode
Whitehaven
The Country Wife Othello Vanity Fair
Winchester
The Country Wife Vanity Fair Macbeth The Tempest
Philoctetes Lady Betty Sara Hamlet As You Like It
Windsor
Vanity Fair
Withernsea
Vanity Fair
Worthing
A Family Affair Sara As You Like It
Wuerzburg
Twelfth Night

York
Macbeth As You Like It

Zutphen
Gotcha & Rack Abbey
Zwolle
Gotcha & Rack Abbey

Australia

Bangladesh
Belgium
Brazil
Bulgaria

Czechoslovakia

Denmark

Egypt
Eire
England

Finland
France

Germany
Greece

Holland
Hong Kong

India
Israel
Italy

Japan

Luxembourg

Malaysia

Nepal
New Zealand
Northern Ireland

Norway

Pakistan
Poland

Romania

Scotland
Singapore
Spain
Sri Lanka

Turkey

Uruguay
USA

Wales

1983
Vanity Fair
Scotsman Fringe First
Scottish Arts Club Award
(Declan Donnellan & Nick Ormerod)

1985
Vanity Fair, Pericles & Andromache
Laurence Olivier Award:
'Most Promising Newcomer'

1986
A Midsummer Night's Dream
Laurence Olivier Award Nominations:
'Comedy of the Year'
'Director of the Year' (Declan Donnellan)

1987
Twelfth Night
Drama Magazine Best Director
(Declan Donnellan)
Time Out Readers' Award (Hugh Ross)
Laurence Olivier Award Nomination:
'Comedy of the Year'

Philoctetes
LWT Plays on Stage Competition: 1st Prize

The Cid, Twelfth Night & Macbeth
Laurence Olivier Award:
'Director of the Year' (Declan Donnellan)

1988
A Family Affair, The Tempest & Philoctetes
Laurence Olivier Award Nomination:
'Designer of the Year' (Nick Ormerod)

A Family Affair
Laurence Olivier Award Nominations:
'Comedy Performance of the Year'
(Lesley Sharp)
'For Outstanding Achievement, in memory of
Kenneth Tynan' (Nick Dear)

1989
Cheek by Jowl
Prudential Award for Theatre: Commendation

1990
Declan Donnellan
Laurence Olivier Award:
'For Outstanding Achievement, in memory of
Kenneth Tynan'
City Limits' best Bald Director
of the Eighties

SELECT BIBLIOGRAPHY

Berry, Ralph *On Directing Shakespeare* (Hamish Hamilton 1989)
Blake, William *The Marriage of Heaven & Hell* (OUP 1975)
Callow, Simon *Being an Actor* (Methuen 1984)
Cook, Judith *Directors' Theatre* (Hodder & Stoughton 1989)
Coveney, Michael *The Citz* (Nick Hern Books 1990)
Drakakis, John (ed) *Alternative Shakespeares* (Methuen 1985)
Edgar, David *The Second Time as Farce* (Lawrence & Wishart 1988)
Gooch, Steve *All Together Now* (Methuen 1984)
Holderness, Graham (ed) *The Shakespeare Myth* (MUP 1988)
Matthews, Barbara *Exhibit A: A Real Live Arts Manager* (Barbara Matthews 1989)
Ritchie, Rob (ed) *The Joint Stock Book* (Methuen 1987)
Shared Experience (Shared Experience 1985)
Stafford-Clark, Max *Letters to George* (Nick Hern Books 1989)
Tynan, Kathleen *The Life of Kenneth Tynan* (Methuen 1988)
Walker, Timothy *Potent Art* (Timothy Walker 1989)

The Art of Success (Methuen 1989)
The Last Days of Don Juan (Absolute Classics 1990)
Our Country's Good (Methuen 1988)
Serious Money (Methuen 1987)
Top Girls (Methuen 1982)

PLAYTEXTS

Restoration Plays (Dent 1976)
Vanity Fair (Declan Donnellan & Nick Ormerod 1982)
Andromache (David Bryer 1984)
Landmarks of French Classical Drama (Methuen 1991)
A Family Affair (Absolute Classics 1989)
Sophocles Plays 2 (Methuen 1990)
The Surgeon of his Honour (University of Wisconsin Press)
Lady Betty (Declan Donnellan & Paddy Cunneen 1989)
Sara (Absolute Classics 1990)

Rack Abbey (Stichting Wikor 1982)
Fuente Ovejuna (Absolute Classics 1989)
Peer Gynt (Nick Hern Books 1990)

The Big Fish (Declan Donnellan & Nick Ormerod 1991)

PHOTOGRAPHS AND ILLUSTRATION CREDITS

INDEX